The World According To Bob

The World According To Bob

JAMES BOWEN

HODDER

First published in Great Britain in 2013 by Hodder & Stoughton
An Hachette UK company

First published in paperback in 2014

12

A CIP catalogue record for this title is available from the British Library

ISBN 978 1 444 77757 4

Printed and bound by CPI Group (UK) Ltd, Croydon, CR0 4YY

Hodder & Stoughton policy is to use papers that are natural, renewable
and recyclable products and made from wood grown in sustainable
forests. The logging and manufacturing processes are expected to
conform to the environmental regulations of the country of origin.

Hodder & Stoughton Ltd
338 Euston Road
London NW1 3BH

www.hodder.co.uk

For all those who devote their lives to helping the homeless and animals in distress

Contents

There is something about the presence of a cat . . .
that seems to take the bite out of being alone.

Louis Camuti

If man could be crossed with the cat, it would improve
man but deteriorate the cat.

Mark Twain

Chapter 1

The Nightwatchman

It had been one of those days, the type where anything that could go wrong had gone wrong.

It had begun when my alarm had failed to go off and I'd overslept which meant that my cat, Bob, and I were already running late when we set off to catch the bus near my flat in Tottenham, north London on our way to Islington, where I sold the homeless magazine *The Big Issue*. We were barely five minutes into our journey when things went from bad to worse.

Bob was sitting in his usual position, half-asleep on the seat next to me when he suddenly lifted his head, looking around suspiciously. In the two years since I'd met him, Bob's ability to sniff trouble had been pretty near infallible. Within moments the bus was filled with an acrid, burning smell and the panicked driver was announcing that our journey was being 'terminated' and we all had to get off. 'Immediately.'

It wasn't quite the evacuation of the *Titanic*, but the bus was three quarters full so there was a lot of chaotic pushing and jostling. Bob didn't seem in a rush so we left them to it and were among the last to get off, which, as it turned out, was a wise decision. The bus may have smelled awful, but at least it was warm.

We had come to a halt opposite a new building site from where icy winds were whipping in at a rate of knots. I was glad that, while dashing out of my flat, I'd hurriedly wrapped a particularly thick, woollen scarf around Bob's neck.

The crisis turned out to be nothing more serious than an overheated engine but the driver had to wait for a bus company mechanic to fix it. So, amid much grumbling and complaining, about two dozen of us were left standing on the freezing cold pavement for almost half an hour while we waited for a replacement bus.

The late morning traffic was terrible, so by the time Bob and I hopped off at our destination, Islington Green, we had been on the road for more than an hour and a half. We were now seriously late. I was going to miss the lunchtime rush, one of the most lucrative times for selling the magazine.

As usual, the five minute walk to our pitch at Angel tube station was a stop-start affair. It always was when I had Bob with me. Sometimes I walked with him on a leather lead, but more often than not we travelled with him perched on my shoulders, gazing curiously out at the world, like the lookout on the prow of a ship. It wasn't something people were used to seeing every day of the week, so we could never walk more than ten yards without someone wanting to say hello and stroke him, or take a photograph. That didn't bother me at all. He was a charismatic, striking-looking fellow and I knew he relished the attention, provided it was friendly. Unfortunately, that wasn't something that could be guaranteed.

The first person to stop us today was a little Russian lady who clearly knew as much about handling cats as I did about reciting Russian poetry.

'Oh, *koschka*, so pretty,' she said, collaring us in Camden Passage, the alleyway of restaurants, bars and antique shops that runs along the southern part of Islington Green. I stopped to let her say hello properly, but she immediately reached up to Bob and tried to touch him on the nose. Not a clever move.

Bob's instant reaction was to lash out, fending her off with a wild wave of his paw and a very loud and emphatic *eeeeeow*. Fortunately he didn't scratch the lady, but he did leave her a little shaken so I had to spend a few minutes making sure she was all right.

'It OK, it OK. I only want to be friend,' she said, looking as white as a sheet. She was quite elderly and I was worried that she might keel over from a heart attack. 'You should never do that to an animal, Madam,' I told her, smiling and being as polite as possible. 'How would you react if someone tried to put their hands on your face? You're lucky he didn't scratch you.'

'I no mean to upset him,' she said.

I felt a bit sorry for her.

'Come on you two, let's be friends,' I said, trying to act as the peacemaker.

Bob was reluctant at first. He'd made his mind up. But he eventually relented, allowing her to run her hand, very gently, along the back of his neck. The lady was very apologetic – and very hard to shake off.

'I very sorry, very sorry,' she kept saying.

'No problem,' I said, by now desperate to get going.

When we finally extricated ourselves and got to the tube station I put my rucksack on the pavement so that Bob could spread out on it – our regular routine – then started laying out the stack of magazines I'd bought from the local *The Big Issue* co-ordinator on Islington Green the previous day. I'd set myself a target of selling at least a couple of dozen today because, as usual, I needed the money.

I was soon being frustrated again.

Ominous, steely clouds had been hovering above London since mid-morning and before I'd managed to sell a single magazine the heavens opened, forcing Bob and me to take shelter a few yards away from our pitch, in an underpass near a bank and some office buildings.

Bob is a resilient creature, but he really hates the rain, especially when it was of the freezing cold variety like today. He almost seemed to shrink in it. His bright marmalade coloured coat also seemed to turn a little bit greyer and less noticeable. Unsurprisingly, fewer people than usual stopped to make a fuss over him so I sold fewer magazines than usual too.

With the rain showing no sign of relenting, Bob was soon making it clear that he didn't want to hang around. He kept shooting me withering looks and, like some kind of ginger hedgehog, scrunched himself up into a ball. I got the message, but knew the reality. The weekend was approaching and I needed to make enough money to keep us both going. But my stack of magazines was still as thick as when I'd arrived.

As if the day wasn't going badly enough, midway through the afternoon a young, uniformed police officer started giving me grief. It wasn't the first time and I knew it wouldn't be the last, but I really didn't need the hassle today. I knew the law; I was perfectly entitled to sell magazines here. I had my registered vendor ID and unless I was causing a public nuisance, I could sell magazines at this spot from dawn 'til dusk. Sadly, he didn't seem to have anything better to do with his day and insisted on searching me. I had no idea what he was frisking me for, presumably drugs or a dangerous weapon, but he found neither.

He wasn't too pleased about that so he resorted to asking questions about Bob. I explained that he was legally registered to me and was micro-chipped. That seemed to worsen his mood even more and he walked off with a look almost as grim as the weather.

I'd persevered for a few more hours but by early evening, when the office workers had gone home and the streets were beginning to fill with drink-ers and kids looking for trouble, I decided to call it quits.

I felt deflated; I'd barely sold ten magazines and collected only a fraction of what I'd normally expect to make. I'd spent long enough living off tins of reduced price beans and even cheaper loaves of bread to know that I wouldn't starve. I had enough money to top up the gas and electric meters and buy a meal or two for Bob as well. But it meant I'd probably need to head out to work again over the weekend, something I really hadn't wanted to do, mainly because there was more rain forecast and I'd been feeling under the weather myself.

As I sat on the bus home, I could feel the first signs of flu seeping into my bones. I was aching and having hot flushes. *Great, that's all I need*, I thought, easing myself deep into my bus seat and settling down to a nap.

By now the sky had turned an inky black and the streetlights were on full blaze. There was something about London at night that fascinated Bob. As I drifted in and out of sleep, he sat there staring out of the window, lost in his own world.

The traffic back to Tottenham was just as bad as it had been in the morning and the bus could only crawl along at a snail's pace. Somewhere past Newington Green, I must have dropped off to sleep completely.

I was woken by the sensation of something lightly tapping me on the leg and the feeling of whiskers brushing against my cheek. I opened my eyes to see Bob with his face close to mine, patting me on the knee with his paw.

'What is it?', I said, slightly grumpily.

He just tilted his head as if pointing towards the front of the bus. He then started making a move off the seat towards the aisle, throwing me slightly concerned glances as he did so.

'Where are you off to?', I was about to ask, but

then I looked out on to the street and realised where we were.

'Oh, sh*t,' I said, jumping up out of my seat immediately.

I grabbed my rucksack and hit the stop button just in the nick of time. Thirty seconds later and it would have been too late. If it hadn't been for my little nightwatchman, we'd have flown past our bus stop.

On the way home I popped into the convenience store on the corner of our road and bought myself some cheap flu remedy tablets. I also got Bob some nibbles and a pouch of his favourite chicken dinner – it was the least I could do, after all. It had been a miserable day and it would have been easy to feel sorry for myself. But, back in the warmth of my little, one-bedroomed flat, watching Bob wolfing down his food, I realised that, actually, I had no real cause to complain. If I'd stayed asleep on the bus much longer I could easily have ended up miles away. Looking out the window, I could see that the weather was, if anything, getting worse. If I'd been out in this rain I could easily have developed something a lot worse than mild flu. I'd had a fortunate escape.

I knew I was lucky in a more profound way, as well. There's an old saying that a wise man is some- one who doesn't grieve for the things which he doesn't have but is grateful for the good things that he does have.

After dinner, I sat on the sofa, wrapped in a blanket sipping a hot toddy of honey, lemon and hot water topped up with a tiny shot of whisky from an old miniature I had lying around. I looked at Bob snoozing contentedly in his favourite spot near the radiator, the troubles of earlier in the day long forgotten. In that moment he couldn't have been happier. I told myself that I should view the world the same way. At this moment in my life, there were so many good things for which I had to be grateful.

It was now a little over two years since I had found Bob, lying injured on the ground floor of this same block of flats. When I'd spotted him in the dingy light of the hallway, he'd looked like he'd been attacked by another animal. He had wounds on the back of his legs and on his body.

At first I'd imagined he belonged to someone else, but – after seeing him in the same place for a few days – I'd taken him up to my flat and nursed him back to health. I'd had to fork out almost every penny I had to buy him medication, but it had been worth it. I'd really enjoyed his company and we'd formed an instant bond.

I'd assumed that it would be a short-lived relationship. He appeared to be a stray so I just naturally assumed that he'd return to the streets. But he'd refused to leave my side. Each day I'd put him outside and try to send him on his way and each day he'd follow me down the road or pop up in the hallway in the evening, inviting himself in for the night. They say that cats choose you, not the other way around. I realised he'd chosen me when he followed me to the bus stop a mile or so away on Tottenham High Road one day. We were far from home so when I'd shooed him away and watched him disappear into the busy crowds, I'd imagined that was the last I'd see of him. But as the bus was pulling away he appeared out of nowhere, leaping on board in a blur of ginger, plonking himself down on the seat next to me. And that had been that.

Ever since then we'd been inseparable, a pair of lost souls eking out an existence on the streets of London.

I suspected that we were actually kindred spirits, each of us helping the other to heal the wounds of our troubled pasts. I had given Bob companionship, food and somewhere warm to lay his head at night and in return he'd given me a new hope and purpose in life. He'd blessed my life with loyalty, love and humour as well as a sense of responsibility I'd never felt before. He'd also given me some goals and helped me see the world more clearly than I had done for a long, long time.

For more than a decade I'd been a drug addict, sleeping rough in doorways and homeless shelters or in basic accommodation around London. For large chunks of those lost years I was oblivious to the world, out of it on heroin, anaesthetised from the loneliness and pain of my everyday life.

As a homeless person I'd become invisible as far as most people were concerned. So as a result, I'd forgotten how to function in the real world and how to interact with people in a lot of situations. In a way I'd been dehumanised. I'd been dead to the world. With Bob's help, I was slowly coming back to life. I'd made huge strides in kicking my drug habit, weaning myself off heroin and then methadone. I was still on medication but could see the light at the end of the tunnel and hoped to be completely clean soon.

It wasn't plain sailing, far from it. It never is for a recovering addict. I still had a habit of taking two steps forward and one step back, and working on the streets didn't help in that respect. It wasn't an environment that was exactly overflowing with the milk of human kindness. Trouble was always around the corner, or it seemed to be for me, at least. I had a knack for attracting it. I always had done.

The truth was that I desperately longed to get off those streets and put that life behind me. I had no idea when or how that was going to be possible, but I was determined to try.

For now, the important thing was to appreciate what I had. By most people's standards, it didn't seem like much. I never had a lot of money and I didn't live in a flashy apartment or have a car. But my life was in a much better place than it had been in the recent past. I had my flat and my job selling *The Big Issue*. For the first time in years I was heading in the right direction – and I had Bob to offer me friendship and to guide me on my way.

As I picked myself up and headed to bed for an early night, I leaned over and gave him a gentle ruffle on the back of his neck.

'Where the hell would I be without you little fella?'

Chapter 2
New Tricks

We are all creatures of habit, and Bob and I are no different to anyone else. Our days together begin with a familiar routine. Some people start their mornings listening to the radio, others with their exercises or a cup of tea or coffee. Bob and I start ours by playing games together.

The moment I wake and sit up, he shuffles out of his bed in the corner of the bedroom, walks over to my side of the bed and starts staring at me inquisitively. Soon after that he starts making a chirruping noise, a bit like a phone. *Brrrr, brrrr.*

If that doesn't gain my full attention he starts making another noise, a slightly more plaintive and pleading noise, a kind of *waaaah*. Sometimes he places his paws on the side of the mattress and hauls himself up so that he is almost at eye-level with me.

He then dabs a paw in my direction, almost as if to nudge me into recognising his message: 'don't ignore me! I've been awake for ages and I'm hungry, so where's my breakfast?' If my response is too slow, he sometimes steps up the charm offensive and does what I call a 'Puss in Boots'. Like the character in the *Shrek* movies, he stands there on the mattress staring at me wide-eyed with his piercing green eyes. It is heartbreakingly cute – and totally irresistible. It always makes me smile. And it always works.

I always keep a packet of his favourite snacks in a drawer by the side of the bed. Depending on how I am feeling, I might let him come up on the bed for a cuddle and a couple of treats or, if I am in a more playful mood, I'll throw them on to the carpet for him to chase around. I often spend the first few minutes of the day lobbing mini treats around, watching him hunt them down. Cats are amazingly agile creatures and Bob often intercepts them in mid-flight, like a cricketer or baseball player fielding a ball in the outfield. He leaps up and catches them in his paws. He has even caught them in his mouth a couple of times. It is quite a spectacle.

On other occasions, if I am tired or not in the mood for playing, he'll entertain himself.

One summer's morning, for instance, I was lying on my bed watching breakfast television. It was shaping up to be a really warm day and it was especially hot up on the fifth floor of our tower block.

Bob was curled up in a shady spot in the bedroom, seemingly fast asleep. Or so I'd assumed.

Suddenly he sat up, jumped on the bed and, almost using it as a trampoline, threw himself at the wall behind me, hitting it quite hard with his paws.

'Bob, what the hell?' I said, gobsmacked. I looked at the duvet and saw a little millipede lying there. Bob was eyeing it and was clearly ready to crunch it in his mouth.

'Oh, no you don't mate,' I said, knowing that insects can be poisonous to cats. 'You don't know where that's been.'

He shot me a look as if to say 'spoilsport'.

I have always been amazed at Bob's speed, strength and athleticism. Someone suggested to me once that he must be related to a Maine Coon or a lynx or some kind of wild cat. It is entirely possible. Bob's past is a complete mystery to me. I don't know how old he is and know nothing about the life he led before I found him. Unless I did a DNA test on him, I'll never know where he comes from or who his parents were. To be honest though, I don't really care. Bob is Bob. And that is all I need to know.

I wasn't the only one who had learned to love Bob for being his colourful, unpredictable self.

It was the spring of 2009 and by now Bob and I had been selling *The Big Issue* for a year or so. Initially we'd had a pitch outside Covent Garden tube station in central London. But we'd moved to Angel, Islington where we'd carved out a little niche for ourselves and Bob had built up a small, but dedicated band of admirers.

As far as I was aware, we were the only human/ feline team selling *The Big Issue* in London. And even if there was another one, I suspected the feline part of the partnership wasn't much competition for Bob when it came to drawing – and pleasing – a crowd.

During our early days together, when I had been a busker playing the guitar and singing, he had sat there, Buddha-like, watching the world going about its business. People were fascinated – and I think a bit mesmerised – by him and would stop, stroke and talk to him. Often they'd ask our story and I'd tell them all about how we'd met and formed our partnership. But that was about the extent of it.

Since we'd been selling *The Big Issue*, however, he'd become a lot more active. I often sat down on the pavement to play with him and we'd developed a few tricks.

It had begun with Bob entertaining people on

his own. He loved to play, so I'd bring along little toys that he would toss around and chase. His favourite was a little grey mouse that had once been filled with catnip.

The mouse had ceased to have any trace of catnip a long time ago and was now a battered, bedraggled and rather pathetic looking thing. Its stitching had begun to come apart and, although it had always been grey, it had now become a really dirty shade of grey. He had loads of other toys, some of which had been given to him by admirers. But 'scraggedy mouse', as I called it, was still his number one toy.

As we sat outside Angel tube he would hold it in his mouth, flicking it from side to side. Sometimes he'd whirl it around by its tail and release it so that it flew a couple of feet away and then pounce on it and start the whole process all over again. Bob loved hunting real life mice, so he was obviously mimicking that. It always stopped people in their tracks and I'd known some commuters to spend ten minutes standing there, as if hypnotised by Bob and his game.

Out of boredom more than anything else, I had started playing with him on the pavement. To begin with we just played at shaking hands. I'd stretch out my hand and Bob would extend his paw to hold it. We were only replicating what we did at home in my flat, but people seemed to find it sweet.

They were constantly stopping to watch us, often taking pictures. If I'd had a pound for every time someone – usually a lady – had stopped and said something like 'aah, how sweet' or 'that's adorable' I'd have been rich enough to, well, not have to sit on the pavement any more.

Freezing your backside off on the streets isn't exactly the most fun you can have, so my playtimes with Bob became more than simple entertainment for the passing crowds. It helped me to pass the time and to enjoy my days a little more too. I couldn't deny it: it also helped encourage people to buy copies of the magazine. It was another one of the blessings that Bob had bestowed on me.

❧

We'd spent so many hours outside Angel by now that we'd begun to develop our act a little further.

Bob loved his little treats, and I learned that he'd go to extraordinary lengths to get hold of them. So, for instance, if I held a little biscuit three feet or so above him, he'd stand on his hind legs in an effort to snaffle the snack from my hands. He would wrap his paws around my wrist to steady himself, then let go with one paw and try to grab it.

Predictably, this had gone down a storm. By now there must have been hundreds of people walking the streets of London with images of Bob reaching for the sky on their telephones and cameras.

Recently, we'd developed this trick even more. The grip he exerted when he grabbed my arms to reach the treat was as strong as a vice. So every now and again I would slowly and very gently raise him in the air so that he was dangling a few inches above the ground.

He would hang there for a few seconds, until he let go and dropped down or I eased him back to earth. I always made sure he had a soft landing of course and usually put my rucksack under him.

The more of a 'show' we put on, the more people seemed to respond to us, and the more generous they became, not just in buying *The Big Issue*.

Since our early days at Angel, people had been incredibly kind, dropping off snacks and nibbles not just for Bob, but for me as well. But they had also started giving us items of clothing, often hand-knitted or sewn by them.

Bob now had a collection of scarves in all sorts of colours. So many, in fact, that I was running out of space to keep them all. He must have had two dozen or more! He was fast becoming to scarves what Imelda Marcos had been to shoes.

It was a little overwhelming at times to know that we were on the receiving end of such warmth, support and love. But I never for a moment kidded myself that there weren't those who felt very differently about us. They were never very far away . . .

It was approaching the busiest time of the week, the Friday evening rush hour, and the crowds passing in and out of Angel tube were growing thicker by the minute. While I wheeled around the street trying to sell my stack of magazines, Bob was totally oblivious to the commotion, flapping his tail absent-mindedly from side to side as he lay on my rucksack on the pavement.

It was only when things had died down, around 7pm, that I noticed a lady standing a few feet away from us. I had no idea how long she had been there, but she was staring intently, almost obsessively at Bob.

From the way she was muttering to herself and shaking her head from side to side occasionally, I sensed she disapproved of us somehow. I had no intention of engaging her in conversation, not least because I was too busy trying to sell the last few copies of the magazine before the weekend.

Unfortunately, she had other ideas.

'Young man. Can't you see that this cat is in distress?', she said, approaching us.

Outwardly, she looked like a school teacher, or

even a headmistress, from some upper-class public school. She was middle-aged, spoke in a clipped, cut-glass English accent and was dressed in a scruffy and un-ironed tweed skirt and jacket. Given her manner, however, I doubted very much that any school would have employed her. She was brusque, bordering on the downright aggressive.

I sensed she was trouble, so didn't respond to her. She was obviously determined to pick a fight, however.

'I have been watching you for a while and I can see that your cat is wagging its tail. Do you know what that means?' she said.

I shrugged. I knew she was going to answer her own question in any case.

'It means it's not happy. You shouldn't be exploiting it like this. I don't think you're fit to look after him.'

I'd been around this track so many times since Bob and I had started working the streets together. But I was polite, so instead of telling this lady to mind her own business, I wearily began defending myself once again.

'He's wagging his tail because he's content. If he didn't want to be there, Madam, you wouldn't see him for dust. He's a cat. They choose who they want to be with. He's free to run off whenever he wants.'

'So why is he on a lead?' she shot back, a smug look on her face.

'He's only on a lead here and when we are on the streets. He ran off once and was terrified when he couldn't find me again. I let him off when he goes to do his business. So, again, if he wasn't happy, as you claim, he'd be gone the minute I took the lead off wouldn't he?'

I'd had this conversation a hundred times before and knew that for 99 people out of that 100, this was a rational and reasonable response. But this lady was part of the 1 per cent who were never going to take my word for it. She was one of those dogmatic individuals who believed they were always right and you were always wrong – and even more wrong if you were impertinent enough not to see their point of view.

'No, no, no. It's a well-known fact that if a cat is wagging its tail it is a distress signal,' she said, more animated now. I noticed that her face was quite red. She was flapping her arms and pacing around us rather menacingly.

I could tell Bob was uncomfortable about her; he had an extremely good radar when it came to spotting trouble. He had stood up and begun backing himself towards me so that he was now standing between my legs, ready to jump up if things got out of hand.

One or two other people had stopped, curious to see what the fuss was about so I knew I had witnesses if the lady did or said anything outrageous.

We carried on arguing for a minute or two. I tried to ease her fears by telling her a little about us.

'We've been together for more than two years. He wouldn't have been with me two minutes if I was mistreating him,' I said at one point. But she was intransigent. Whatever I said, she just shook her head and tutted away. She simply wasn't willing to listen to my point of view. It was frustrating in the extreme, but there was nothing more I could do. I resigned myself to the fact that she was entitled to her opinion. 'Why don't we agree to differ?' I said at one point.

'Hffff,' she said, waving her arms at me. 'I'm not agreeing with anything you say young man.'

Eventually, to my huge relief, she started walking away, muttering and shaking her head as she shuffled off into the crowds jostling around the entrance to the tube station.

I watched her for a moment, but was soon distracted by a couple of customers. Fortunately, their attitude was the complete opposite of the one this lady had displayed. Their smiles were a welcome relief.

I was handing one of them their change when I heard a noise behind me that I recognised immediately. It was a loud, piercing *wheeeeow*. I spun round and saw the woman in the tweed suit. Not only had she come back, she was now holding Bob in her arms.

Somehow, while I had been distracted, she had managed to scoop him up off the rucksack. She was now nursing him awkwardly, with no affection or empathy, one hand under his stomach and another on his back. It was strange, as if she'd never picked up an animal before in her life. She could have been holding a joint of meat that she'd just bought at the butcher or a large vegetable at a market.

Bob was clearly furious about being manhandled like this and was wriggling like crazy.

'What the hell do you think you are doing?' I shouted. 'Put him down, right now or I'll call the police.'

'He needs to be taken somewhere safe,' she said, a slightly crazed expression forming on her reddening face.

Oh God no, she's going to run off with him, I said to myself, preparing to drop my supply of magazines and set off in hot pursuit through the streets of Islington.

Luckily, she hadn't quite thought it through because Bob's long lead was still tethered to my rucksack. For a moment there was a kind of stand-off. But then I saw her eye moving along the lead to the rucksack.

'No you don't,' I said, stepping forward to intercept her.

My movement caught her off guard which in

turn gave Bob his chance. He let out another screeching *wheeeeow* and freed himself from the woman's grip. He didn't scratch her but he did dig his paws into her arm which forced her to panic and suddenly drop him on to the pavement.

He landed with a bit of a bump, then stood there for a second growling and hissing and baring his teeth at her. I'd never seen him quite so aggressive towards anyone or anything.

Unbelievably, she used this as an argument against me.

'Ah, look, see, he's angry,' she said, pointing at Bob and addressing the half dozen or more people who were watching events unfold.

'He's angry because you just picked him up without his permission,' I said. 'He only lets me pick him up.'

She wasn't giving up that easily. She clearly felt she had some kind of audience and was going to play to them.

'No, he's angry because of the way you are treating him,' she said. 'Everyone can see that. That's why he should be taken away from you. He doesn't want to be with you.'

Again there was a brief impasse while everyone held their breath to see what happened next. It was Bob who broke the silence.

He gave the woman a really disdainful look, then padded his way back towards me. He began rubbing his head against the outside of my leg, and purring noisily when I put my hand down to stroke him.

He then plonked his rear down on the ground and looked up at me again playfully, as if to say, 'now can we get on with some more tricks?' Recognising the look, I dipped my hand into my coat pocket and produced a treat. Almost immediately, Bob got up on his hind legs and grabbed hold of my arms. I then popped the treat into his mouth drawing a couple of audible *aaahs* from somewhere behind me.

There were times when Bob's intelligence and ability to understand the nuances of what's going on around him defied belief. This was one such moment. Bob had played to the crowd totally. It was as if he had wanted to make a statement. It was as if he was saying: 'I'm with James, and I'm really happy to be with James. And anyone who says otherwise is mistaken. End of story.' That was certainly the message that most of the onlookers got. One or two of them were familiar faces, people who had bought magazines off me in the past or stopped to say hello to Bob. They turned to the woman in the tweed suit and made their feelings plain.

'We know this guy, he's cool,' one young man in a business suit said.

'Yes, leave them alone. They're not doing anyone

any harm and he looks after his cat really well,' another middle-aged lady said. One or two other people made supportive noises. As various other voices chipped in, not one of them backed up the lady in the tweed suit.

The expression that had formed on her face by this point told its own story. She was, by now, even redder than ever, almost purple in fact. She spluttered and grumbled for a moment or two but made no real sense. Clearly the penny had dropped and she realised that she had lost this particular battle. So she turned on her heels and disappeared once more into the crowds, this time – thankfully – permanently.

'You OK, James?' one of the onlookers asked me, as I kneeled down to check on Bob. He was purring loudly but his breathing was steady and there was no sign of any injury from when he was dropped to the ground.

'I'm fine, thanks,' I said, not being entirely honest.

I hated it when people implied I was using Bob in some way. It hurt me deeply. In a way we were victims of our circumstances. Bob wanted to be with me, of that I was absolutely certain. He'd proven that time and time again. Unfortunately, at the moment, that meant that he had to spend his days with me on the streets. Those were the simple facts of my life. I didn't have a choice.

The downside was that this made us easy targets, sitting ducks for people to judge. We were lucky, most people judged us kindly. I had learned to accept that there would always be those who would not.

Chapter 3

The Bobmobile

It was a balmy, early summer afternoon and I had decided to knock off from work early. The sunny weather seemed to have put a smile on everyone's face and I'd reaped the benefits, selling out my supply of magazines in a few hours.

Since I'd started selling *The Big Issue* a couple of years earlier, I'd learned to be sensible, so I'd decided to plough some of the money back into buying some more magazines for the rest of the week. With Bob on my shoulders, I headed over to see Rita, the co-ordinator on the north side of Islington High Street on the way back to catch the bus home.

From a distance, I could see that she was having an animated conversation with a group of vendors in red bibs who were huddled around something. It turned out to be a bicycle. I got on well with Rita, so knew that I could gently take the mickey.

'What's this, Rita?' I joked. 'Riding in the Tour de France?'

'Don't think so, James,' she smiled. 'Someone just sold it to me in exchange for ten magazines. I really don't know what to do with it to be honest. Bikes aren't really my thing.'

It was obvious the bike wasn't in prime condition. There were hints of rust on the handlebars and the light at the front had cracked glass. The paintwork had a few chips and nicks and, just for good measure, one of the mudguards had been snapped in half. Mechanically, though, it looked like it was in reasonable condition.

'Is it roadworthy?' I asked Rita.

'Think so,' she shrugged. 'He muttered something about one of the sets of brakes needing a bit of attention but that's all.'

She could see my mind was working overtime.

'Why don't you give it a try, see what you think?'

'Why not?' I said. 'Can you keep an eye on Bob for a second?'

I was no Bradley Wiggins but I had ridden bikes throughout my childhood and again in London. As part of my rehabilitation a few years earlier, I had been briefly involved with a bicycle building course so I knew a bit about cycle maintenance. It felt good to know some of that training hadn't gone to waste.

Handing Bob's lead to Rita, I took the bike and flipped it upside down to inspect it properly. The tyres were inflated and the chain looked like it was well oiled and moving pretty freely. The seat was a little low for me, so I adjusted it up a little. I then took the bike down on to the road and gave it a quick workout. The gears were a tad on the sticky side and, as Rita had warned me, the front brakes weren't working properly. I had to apply maximum pressure on the handle to get any reaction and even then it wasn't enough to bring the bike to a halt. I figured there was a problem with the wire inside the cable. It was easily fixed I suspected. The rear brakes were fine, however, which was all I needed to know.

'What does that mean?' Rita said when I reported all this back to her.

'It means it's OK to ride,' I said.

By now I'd made a decision.

'Tell you what, I'll give you a tenner for it,' I said.

'Really. You sure?' Rita said, a little taken aback.

'Yes,' I replied.

'OK, deal. You'll need this as well,' she said, fishing around under her trolley and producing a rather battered, old black cycle helmet.

I'd always been a bit of a hoarder, collecting bits and pieces, and for a while my little flat had been full of all sorts of junk, from mannequins to road signs. But this was different. This was actually one of the first, sensible investments I'd made in a while. I knew the bike would be useful back up in Tottenham where I could use it for short journeys to the shops or the doctors. I'd make the £10 back in saved bus fares in no time. For the longer journey to work at Angel or into central London I'd carry on taking the bus or the tube. That journey was too treacherous to cycle because of the main roads and junctions I'd have to negotiate. Some of them were notorious cycling accident spots.

It was only then, as I mentally mapped out the journeys that I'd be able to cycle from now on, that it suddenly struck me.

'Ah, how am I going to get this home?'

Bus drivers don't let bikes on board and there was no prospect of getting it on a tube. I'd be stopped at the barriers immediately. I might get away with taking it on an overground train, but there were no lines that went anywhere near my flats.

There's only thing for it, I told myself.

'OK, Bob, looks like you and I are riding this home,' I said.

Bob had been soaking up the sunshine on the pavement near Rita but had been keeping half an eye on me throughout. When I'd climbed on the bike, he tilted his head to one side slightly, as if to say: 'what's that contraption and why are you sitting on top of it?'

He looked suspiciously at me again as I strapped on the cycle helmet, slung my rucksack on my shoulders and started wheeling the bike towards him.

'Come on, mate, climb on board,' I said, reaching down to him and letting him climb on my shoulders.

'Good luck,' Rita said.

'Thanks. I think we'll need it!' I said.

The traffic on Islington High Street was heavy and, as usual, at a virtual standstill. So I walked the bike along the pavement for a while, towards Islington Memorial Green. We passed a couple of police officers who gave me a curious look, but said nothing. There was no law against riding a bike with a cat on your shoulders. Well, as far as I was aware there wasn't. I guess if they'd wanted to pull me over they could have done. They obviously had better things to do with their afternoon, thank God.

I didn't want to cycle along the High Street so I wheeled the bike across a pedestrian crossing. We drew more than our fair share of glances; the looks on people's faces ranged from astonishment to hilarity. More than one person stopped in their tracks, pointing at us as if we were visitors from another planet.

We didn't linger and cut across the corner of the Green, past the Waterstones bookshop, and turned into the main road to north London, Essex Road.

'OK, here we go, Bob,' I said, bracing myself to enter the heavy traffic. We were soon weaving our way through the buses, vans, cars and lorries.

Bob and I soon got the hang of it. As I focussed

on staying upright, I could feel him re-adjusting himself. Rather than standing he decided, sensibly, to drape himself across my neck, with his head down low and pointing forward. He clearly wanted to settle down and enjoy the ride.

It was mid-afternoon and a lot of children were heading home from school. All along Essex Road groups of kids in uniforms would stop and wave at us. I tried waving back at one point but lost my balance a little bit, sending Bob sliding down my shoulder.

'Oops, sorry, mate. Won't do that again,' I said, as we both regained our equilibrium.

Progress was steady but a little slow at times. If we had to stop because of traffic we were instantly shouted at by someone asking for a photo. At one point, two teenage schoolgirls jumped out into the road to snap themselves with us.

'Oh my God, this is so cute,' one of them said, leaning into us so heavily as she posed for her photo that she almost knocked us over.

I hadn't ridden a bicycle for a few years and I wasn't exactly in prime physical condition. So I took a little breather every now and again, attracting a posse of onlookers each time I did so. Most smiled their approval but a couple shook their heads disapprovingly.

'Stupid idiot,' I heard one middle-aged guy in a suit say as he strode past us.

It didn't feel stupid at all. In fact, it felt rather fun. And I could tell Bob was having a good time too. His head was right next to mine and I could feel him purring contentedly in my ear.

We travelled all the way down to Newington Green and from there towards Kingsland Road where the road headed down towards Seven Sisters. I had been looking forward to this section. For most of the journey, apart from a couple of little inclines here and there, the road had been fairly flat. At that point, however, I knew that it dropped downhill for a mile or so. I'd be able to freewheel down it quite easily.

To my delight, I saw there was a dedicated bike lane, which was completely empty. Bob and I were soon flying down the hill, the warm summer air blowing through our hair. 'Woohoo. Isn't this great Bob?,' I said at one point. I felt a bit like Elliott in E.T. – not that I expected us to take off and fly our way back across the north London rooftops at any point, obviously, but we must have been clocking close to 20 miles per hour at one point.

The traffic in the main lane to our right was grid-locked, and people were winding down their windows to let in some air. Some of the expressions on their faces as we whizzed past them were priceless.

A couple of children stuck their heads out of the sun roofs of their cars and shouted at us. A few people just looked on in utter disbelief. It was understandable, I supposed. You don't see a ginger cat whizzing down a hill on a bike very often.

It only took me about half an hour to get home, which was pretty impressive considering we'd had so many unplanned stops.

As we pulled up in the communal area outside the flats, Bob just hopped off my shoulders as if he was disembarking the bus. This was typical of his laid-back attitude to life. He had taken it all in his stride; just another routine day in London.

Back in the flat, I spent the rest of the afternoon and evening tinkering with the bike. I'd soon fixed the front brakes and given it a general tuning up.

'There you go,' I said to Bob, as I stood back to admire my handiwork. 'I think we've got ourselves a Bobmobile.'

I couldn't be sure, but I was pretty sure that the look he gave me signalled his approval.

People often ask me how Bob and I communicate with each other so well.

'It's simple,' I usually answer. 'He has his own language, and I've learned to understand it.'

It might sound far-fetched, but it's true.

His main means of communication is body

language. He has a range of signals that tell me exactly what he is feeling, and more to the point, what he wants at any particular moment. For instance, if he wants to go to the toilet, when we are walking around the streets, he starts grumbling and growling a little bit. He then starts fidgeting on my shoulder. I don't need to look at him to know what he is up to; he's scouting around for a spot with some soft dirt where he can do his business.

If, on the other hand, he is walking on his lead and gets tired he lets out a light, low-pitched grumble or moan-cum-growl. He also refuses to walk an inch. He just looks at me as if to say 'come on mate, pick me up I'm worn out'.

If he ever gets scared he backs up on my shoulder, or if he is standing on the floor, he performs a reverse manoeuvre so that he is standing between my legs in position in case I need to pick him up. To his credit, it is rare that anything frightens him. The sound of an ambulance or a police car going by with their sirens blaring barely bothers him at all. He is very used to it, living and working in central London. The only thing that freaks him a little is the pressurised air brakes on big lorries and buses. Whenever he hears that loud, hissing sound he recoils and looks scared. On bonfire nights, he also gets a little nervous about the loud bangs and explosions, but he generally enjoys watching the bright, sparkling lights in the sky from the window of my flat.

There are other signals too. For instance, I can tell a lot about his mood from the way he moves his tail. If he is snoozing or asleep his tail is still and quiet, of course. But at other times he wags it around, using different movements. The most common wag is a gentle side-to-side movement, rather like a windscreen wiper on its slowest setting. This is his contentment wag. I've spent endless hours sitting around London with him and have seen him doing it when he is being entertained or intrigued by something. The lady who'd tried to steal him at Angel hadn't been the first to misread this movement. Others had made the same mistake and misconstrued it as a sign of anger. Bob does get angry, but he signals that with a very different tail movement in which he flicks it around, a bit like a fly swatter.

There are subtler messages too. If, for instance, he is worried about me, he comes up really close as if to examine me. If I am feeling under the weather, he often sidles up and listens to my chest. He does a lot of loving things like that. He has this habit of coming up and rubbing against me, purring. He also rubs his face on my hand tilting his head so that I can scratch behind his ear. Animal behaviourists and zoologists are entitled to their opinions, but to me this is Bob's way of telling me that he loves me.

Of course, the most frequent message he wants to get across relates to food. If he wants me to come to the kitchen to feed him, for instance, he goes around banging on the doors. He is so clever, he could easily unpick one of the child locks I've had to fit specifically to keep him out, so I always have to go and check. By the time I get there, he has always removed himself to a spot by the radiator in the corner where he'll be wearing his most innocent look. But that doesn't last for long and he'll soon be pleading for a snack.

Bob is nothing if not persistent and won't leave me alone until he gets what he wants. He can get quite frustrated if I choose to ignore him and tries all sorts of tricks from tapping me on the knee to giving me the 'Puss in Boots' look. There is no end to his creativity when it comes to filling a gap in his tummy.

For a while, his biggest challenge was distracting me while I played computer games on the second-hand Xbox I'd picked up in a charity shop. Most of the time Bob was quite happy to watch me playing. He was fascinated by certain games, especially motor racing ones. He would stand beside me experiencing each bend and manoeuvre. On one occasion, I could have sworn I saw his body swaying as we took a particularly sharp hairpin bend together. He drew the line at action games with a lot of shooting, however. If I was playing one of these he would carry himself off to another corner of the room. If the game – or I – ever got too loud he'd lift up his head and look across. The message was simple: 'turn it down please, can't you see I'm trying to snooze'.

I could get really wrapped up in a game. It wasn't unheard of for me to start a game at 9pm and not finish until the wee small hours. But Bob didn't appreciate this and would do his damnedest to get my attention, especially when he was hungry.

There were times, however, when I was immune to his charms so he took more drastic measures.

I was playing a game with Belle one night when Bob appeared. He'd had dinner a couple of hours earlier and had decided that he needed a snack. He went through his usual attention-seeking routine, making a selection of noises, draping himself across my feet and rubbing himself against my legs. But we were both so heavily involved in reaching the next level of this game that we didn't respond at all.

He sloped off for a moment, circling the area where the TV and Xbox were plugged in. After a moment, he moved in towards the control console and pressed his head against the big, touch sensitive button in the middle.

'Bob, what are you up to?' I asked innocently, still too engrossed in the game to twig what he was doing.

A moment later, the screen went black and the

Xbox started powering down. He had applied enough pressure to the button that he'd switched it off. We had been halfway through a really tricky level of the game, so should have been furious with him. But we both sat there with the same expression of disbelief on our faces.

'Did he just do what I think he did?' Belle asked me.

'Well, I saw it too, so he must have. But I don't believe it.'

Bob stood there looking triumphant. His expression said it all: 'So how are you going to ignore me now?'

We don't always rely on signals and body language. There are times when we have a strange kind of telepathy, as if we both know what the other one is thinking, or doing. We've also learned to alert each other to danger.

A few days after I'd acquired the bike, I decided to take Bob to a local park that had just been given a bit of a makeover. By now he was completely comfortable riding around on my shoulders and had become more and more confident, leaning in and out of the corners like a motorbike pillion rider.

The park turned out to be a bit of a disappointment. Apart from a few new benches and shrubs and a decent playground for young children, it seemed nothing much had changed. Bob was keen to explore, nevertheless. If I felt it was safe, I occasionally let him off his lead so that he could enjoy himself scrabbling around in the overgrowth while he did his business. I had just done so today and was sitting, reading a comic and soaking up a few rays of sunshine, when, in the distance, I heard the barking of a dog.

Uh oh, I thought.

At first, I guessed it was a couple of streets away. But as the barking grew louder I realised it was a lot closer than that. In the distance I saw a very large, and very menacing looking, German Shepherd running towards the entrance to the park. The dog was no more than 150 yards away and was off its leash. I could tell it was looking for trouble.

'Bob,' I shouted at the overgrowth where, I knew, he was busy conducting his call of nature. 'Bob, come here.'

For a moment, I was panic stricken. But, as so often in the past, we were on the same wavelength and his head soon popped up in the bushes. I was waving my arms at him, encouraging him to join me without making too much fuss. I didn't want the dog to spot me. Bob understood what was happening immediately and bolted out of the bushes. He wasn't afraid of dogs, but he picked his battles wisely. Judging by the noise the German Shepherd was making, this wasn't a dog with which we wanted to pick a fight.

Bob's bright ginger coat wasn't exactly hard to spot amidst the greenery, though, and the dog soon began accelerating towards us, barking even more fiercely. For a moment I had a terrible feeling that Bob had left it too late so I grabbed the bike and got ready to ride it into the firing line if necessary. I knew if the German Shepherd intercepted him, Bob could be in serious trouble.

As so often in the past, however, I'd underestimated him.

He sprinted across the grass and arrived as I crouched down on one knee. In one seamless move, I flipped him on to my shoulder, jumped straight on to the bike, and – with Bob standing on my shoulders – hit the pedals and began cycling out of the park.

The frustrated German Shepherd pursued us for a short time, at one point running alongside as we sped down the street. I could hear Bob hissing at him. I couldn't see his face, but it wouldn't have surprised me at all if he was taunting him.

'What are you going to do about it now, tough guy?' he was probably saying.

As I hit the main road back towards our block of flats, I looked round to see our nemesis receding

into the distance where he had been joined by his
owner, a big, burly guy in a black jacket and jeans.
He was struggling to get the dog back on its lead,
but that was his problem, not mine.

'That was a close one, Bob,' I said. 'Thank goodness for the Bobmobile.'

Chapter 4

The Odd Couple

It was rare I got visitors at the flat. I didn't have many friends locally and kept to myself within the building. I would pass the time of day with neighbours but I could count the number of times any of them had popped round for a chat on the fingers of one hand. So I was always wary whenever someone knocked on the door or pressed the building's intercom at the entrance downstairs. I automatically assumed the worst, expecting to find myself confronted by a bailiff or a debt collector chasing me for money that I didn't have.

That was my immediate reaction when the intercom buzzer went just after 9am one weekday morning as Bob and I got ready for work.

'Who the heck is that?' I said, instinctively twitching at the curtains even though I had no view of the entrance from up on the fifth floor.

'James, it's Titch. Can I come up with Princess?' a familiar voice said over the speaker.

'Ah. Titch. Sure, head on up, I'll put the kettle on,' I said, breathing a sigh of relief.

Titch was, as his name suggested, a tiny little bloke. He was wiry and had short, thinning hair. Like me, he was a recovering addict who had started selling *The Big Issue*. He had been having a hard time and had crashed out at my place a couple of times in recent months. He'd got into trouble with work after becoming a co-ordinator in Islington. He had been 'de-badged' and given a six month suspension. He was still waiting for his ban to be lifted and had been really struggling to make ends meet.

I felt like I'd been given a second chance in life since I'd met Bob so had given Titch another opportunity as well. I also quite liked him. Deep down, I knew, he had a good heart.

Another reason that Titch and I got on was that we both worked on the street with our pet as our companion. In Titch's case it was his faithful black Labrador-Staffordshire Bull Terrier-cross, Princess. She was a lovely, sweet-natured dog. When he'd stayed with me previously, he'd left Princess somewhere else. He knew that I had Bob and that having a dog in the house might cause problems for me. But, for some reason, that wasn't the case today. I braced myself for what might happen when the pair of them arrived at the front door.

Bob's ears pricked up at the sound of knocking. When he saw Titch and Princess walking in, his first reaction was to arch his back and hiss. Cats arch their backs to make themselves look bigger in a fight, apparently. This is why they also get their hair to stand on end. In this particular case, however, Bob needn't have bothered. Princess was a really easy-going and affectionate dog. She could also be a little nervous. So the moment she saw Bob in full, confrontational mode she just froze to the spot. It was a complete reversal of the normal roles, where the physically bigger dog intimidates the smaller cat.

'It's all right, Princess,' I said. 'He won't hurt you.'

I then led her into my bedroom and shut the door so that she felt safe.

'James, mate. Is there any way you can look after Princess for the day?' Titch said, cutting straight to the chase when I handed him a mug of tea. 'I've got to go and sort out my social security situation.'

'Sure,' I said, knowing how long those sorts of things could take. 'Shouldn't be a problem. Should it Bob?'

He gave me an enigmatic look.

'We are working at Angel today. She'll be all right with us there won't she?' I said.

'Yeah, no problem,' Titch said. 'So how about if I pick her up there this evening at about 6pm?'

'OK,' I said.

'Right, better dash. Got to be in the front of the queue if I want to be seen this side of Christmas,' Titch said, popping his head into my bedroom.

'Be a good girl, Princess,' he said, before heading off.

As he'd demonstrated again already this morning, Bob didn't have a major problem with dogs unless they were aggressive towards him. Even then, he could handle himself pretty well and had seen off a few scary looking mongrels with a growl and a loud hiss. Back during our early days busking around Covent Garden, I'd even seen him give one over-aggressive dog a bop on the nose with his paw.

Bob wasn't just territorial with dogs. He wasn't a huge fan of other cats, either. There were times when I wondered whether he didn't actually know he was a cat. He seemed to look at them as if they were inferior beings, unfit to breathe the same air as him. Our route to and from work had become more complicated in recent months thanks to the cancellation of a bus service that used to take us straight from Tottenham High Road to Angel. So we'd started taking different buses, one of which required us to change in Newington Green, a mile or so from Angel. When money was tight, we'd walk to Angel. As we did so, Bob would sniff and stare whenever we went past what was clearly a cat house.

If he ever saw another cat out and about he would let them know in no uncertain terms that this was his turf.

Once when he saw a tabby cat, skulking around on Islington Green Bob had been transformed. He had been straining so hard to get at this upstart invading his territory, it had been as if I'd had a particularly aggressive dog on the end of the lead. He'd had to stamp his authority on the situation. Obviously, he'd already felt the need to do the same with Princess.

If I had any reservations, they were that Princess might be a bit of an inconvenience. Dogs were so much more hard work than cats. For a start, you couldn't put them on your shoulders as you walked down the street, a design flaw that, I soon discovered, slowed you down considerably.

Walking to the bus stop Princess was a right royal pain. She pulled on the lead, stopped to sniff random patches of grass and veered off to squat down and go to the toilet no less than three times in the space of a couple of hundred yards.

'Come on Princess, or we'll never get there,' I said, already regretting my decision. Suddenly I remembered why I had never wanted to adopt a dog as a pet.

If I was struggling to establish some kind of control over her, however, Bob had no such trouble. On the bus, he took up his normal position on the seat next to the window, from where he kept a watchful eye on Princess, who was tucked under my feet. Bob's face had always been expressive. The looks he gave Princess whenever she encroached on his territory during the journey were hilarious. The area under the seat wasn't exactly spacious and Princess would occasionally wiggle to improve her position. Each time she did so Bob would give her a look that simply said: 'why don't you sit still you stupid dog?'.

Outside the weather was atrocious, with rain hammering down. Arriving in Islington, I took Bob to the little park at Islington Green to quickly do his business and decided to let Princess do the same. Big mistake. She took forever to find a suitable spot. I then realised I'd forgotten to bring any plastic bags with me so had to fish around in a rubbish bin to find something with which to scoop up her droppings. I really wasn't enjoying my day as a dogsitter, I decided.

With the rain getting heavier by the minute, I took shelter under the canopy of a café. When a waitress appeared I decided I might as well ask her for a cup of tea, a saucer of milk for Bob and some water for Princess. I then popped inside to use the toilet, leaving my two companions tied to the table with their leads.

I only left them for a couple of minutes, but when I got back it was clear that some kind of jostling for position had been going on. I'd left them with Bob sitting on a chair and Princess standing under the table. But when I came back Bob was sitting on the table, lapping at a saucer of milk, while Princess was sitting under the table looking far from happy with her bowl of water. I had no idea what had gone on, but Bob had clearly established himself as the senior partner once again.

As always, Bob was also attracting attention from passers-by. Despite the weather, a couple of ladies stopped to stroke him and say hello. But poor Princess was hardly even acknowledged. It was as if she wasn't even there. In a funny way, I knew how she felt. I live in Bob's shadow sometimes.

The rain eventually eased off and we headed towards Angel and our pitch. While Bob and I took up our usual positions, Princess lay down a few feet away with her head deliberately placed so that she could take in most of the scene around us. Part of me had thought she'd be a burden but it turned out to be quite the opposite: she proved to be rather a useful asset.

As I paced around trying to persuade passers-by to fork out a couple of quid for a magazine, Princess sat there attentively, her head on the pavement and her eyes swivelling around like surveillance cameras, carefully weighing up everyone who approached us. If they got her seal of approval, she remained rooted to the spot, but if she had any suspicions she would suddenly sit upright ready to intervene. If she didn't like the cut of someone's jib she would let out a little growl or even a bark. It was usually enough to get the message across.

An hour or so after we'd settled down, a drunk carrying a can of extra strength lager came weaving his way towards us. They could be the bane of my existence at Angel. Almost every day I'd be asked for a quid for a beer by someone off his face on Special Brew. Princess spotted him, stood up and barked a quick warning as if to say 'steer clear'. She wasn't the world's biggest dog, but she looked intimidating enough. She was more Staffie than Lab in that respect. He had soon veered off on another course, heading off to bother someone other poor soul instead.

Princess was at her most alert whenever anyone knelt down to stroke and say hello to Bob. She would take a step towards them, jutting her head forward so that she could make sure that they were treating the smallest member of our trio with the proper respect. Again, if she disapproved of anyone she made her feelings clear and they would stand back.

She actually made my job a little easier. It could often be a challenge to keep an eye on Bob while trying to sell the magazine at the same time, especially when the street was busy. The incident with the lady in the tweed suit had made me especially wary.

'Thank you, Princess,' I began saying on a regular basis, handing her a little treat from my rucksack.

Even Bob shot her a couple of approving looks. Somewhere, deep inside his feline mind I felt sure he was revising his opinion of our unexpected new recruit. *'Maybe she's not so bad after all,'* he may have been thinking.

The weather remained miserable all afternoon, so when the clock started edging towards six, I started looking out for Titch. I'd done pretty well selling magazines and wanted to start heading homewards. It was no night to be out late. But there was no sign of him. Six pm came and went and still there was nothing. I saw one of the *The Big Issue* co-ordinators heading home from work. Everyone knew Titch, so I asked if she'd seen him.

'No, haven't seen him for weeks actually,' she said. 'Not since all that trouble, you know?'

'Yeah,' I said.

By 6.30pm I'd become thoroughly disillusioned. I knew street people weren't the world's greatest timekeepers, but this was getting ridiculous.

'Come on you two, let's head for home. He can come and collect you there, Princess,' I said, gathering all my stuff together. I was cheesed off with Titch, but I was also a little worried. Bob had tolerated Princess being in the flat for a few minutes earlier but having her for a 'sleepover' was another matter altogether. I could foresee lots of barking from Princess, complaints from the neighbours and a sleepless night for me.

I stopped at the convenience store to grab some food for Princess. I had no idea what she liked to eat, so gambled on a tin of standard fare dog food and some doggie biscuits.

Back in the kitchen as we all settled down to dinner, Bob once more ensured that the pecking order was clear. When Princess made a move towards the bowl of water I'd laid out for her, Bob hissed and snarled loudly, forcing the interloper to back off. He had to lap up his own bowl of milk first.

It didn't take them long to reach an accommodation though. In fact, Bob was so content with his new companion that he allowed her to clear out the remains of his dinner bowl.

I've seen it all now, I thought to myself. Actually, I hadn't.

I was shattered by 10pm and fell asleep in front of the television. When I woke up I saw something that made me wish I owned a video camera. I would have made a small fortune on those television shows that feature cute animal clips.

Bob and Princess were both splayed out on the carpet, snoozing quietly. When I'd left them they were at opposite ends of the room, with Bob near his favourite spot by the radiator and Princess near the door. While I'd been sleeping, Princess had clearly sought out the warmth of the radiator and slid alongside Bob. Her head was now barely a foot from Bob's nose. If I hadn't known any better, I'd have guessed that they were lifelong pals. I locked the front door, switched off the lights and headed off to bed leaving them there. I didn't hear a peep from either of them until the following morning when I was woken up by the sound of barking.

It took me a moment to remember that I had a dog in the house.

'What's wrong, Princess?' I said, still half asleep.

They say that some animals can sense their owners are nearby. My best friend Belle some-times stayed at the flat with us and she had told me that Bob often sensed when I was coming home. Several times he had jumped up on the window sill in the kitchen looking anxiously down to the street below minutes before I arrived at the front door. Princess clearly had the same gift because a couple of moments later I heard the buzzer. It was Titch.

From the look of his unshaven and rather bleary face, he had slept rough, which, knowing Titch, was quite possible.

'Really sorry to leave you in the lurch last night but something came up,' he said, apologetically. I didn't bother asking what it was. I'd had nights like that myself, far too many of them.

I made another cup of tea and stuck some bread in the toaster. He looked like he could do with something warm inside him.

Bob was lying next to the radiator, with Princess curled up a couple of feet away, his eyes once more fixed on his new friend. The expression on Titch's face was priceless. He was dumbstruck.

'Look at those two, they get on like a house on fire now,' I smiled.

'I can see it, but I can't quite believe it,' he said, grinning widely.

Titch wasn't a man to miss an opportunity.

'So would you mind looking after her again if I'm in the lurch?' he asked, munching on his toast.

'Why not?' I said.

Chapter 5

The Ghost on the Stairs

The rain had been relentless for days, transforming the streets of London into miniature paddling pools. Bob and I were regularly returning home soaked to the skin, so today I'd given up and headed home early.

I arrived back at the flats around mid-afternoon desperate to get out of my wet clothes and let Bob warm himself by the radiator.

The lift in my building was erratic at the best of times. After a few minutes repeatedly pressing the button for it to come down from the fifth floor, I realised it was out of order once more.

'Brilliant,' I muttered to myself. 'It's the long walk up again I'm afraid Bob.'

He looked at me forlornly.

'Come on then,' I said, dipping my shoulder down so that he could climb on board.

We were just beginning the final couple of flights of stairs, from the fourth to the fifth floor, when I noticed a figure in the shadows on the landing above us.

'Hold on here for a second, Bob,' I said, placing him down on the steps and heading up on my own.

Moving in closer I could see that it was a man and he was leaning against the wall. He was hunched over with his trousers partially dropped down and there was something metallic in his hand. I knew instantly what he was doing.

In the past, the flats had been notorious as a haunt for drug users and dealers. Addicts would find their way in and use the staircase and hallways to smoke crack and marijuana or inject themselves with heroin like this guy was doing. In the years since I'd moved in, the police had improved the situation dramatically, but we'd still occasionally see young kids dealing in the stairwell on the ground floor. It was nowhere near as bad as a previous sheltered housing project I'd lived in, over in Dalston, which was over-run with crack addicts. But it was still distressing, especially for the families who lived in the flats. No one wants their children arriving home from school to find a junkie shooting up on the staircase outside their home.

For me, of course, it was a reminder of the past I was desperate to put behind me. I continued to struggle with my addiction; I always would. That, unfortunately, was the nature of the beast. But, since teaming up with Bob, I'd made the breakthrough and was on the way to complete recovery. After weaning myself off heroin and then methadone, I'd been prescribed a drug called subutex, a milder medication that was slowly but surely reducing my drug dependency. The counsellor at my drug dependency unit had likened this final part of my recovery to landing an aeroplane: I would slowly drop back down to earth. I'd been on subutex for several months now. The landing gear was down and I could see the lights of the runway in front of me. The descent was going according to plan, I was almost back on solid ground.

I could do without seeing this, I said to myself.

I saw that the guy was in his mid-forties with a short, crew-cut hairstyle. He was wearing a black coat, t-shirt and jeans and a pair of scruffy trainers. Fortunately he wasn't aggressive. In fact he was quite the opposite. He was really apologetic, which was pretty unusual. Selflessness isn't really a strong suit in heroin addicts.

'Sorry, mate, I'll get out of your way,' he said in a thick East End accent, taking his 'works' out of his leg and pulling up his trousers. I could tell that he'd finished injecting. His eyes had that tell-tale glazed look.

I decided to let him go first. I knew better than to

completely trust an addict. I wanted to keep him ahead of me where I could see him.

He was pretty unsteady on his feet and stumbled up the short flight of stairs to the landing on the fifth floor, through the doors and into the hallway heading for the lift.

Bob had trotted up the final flight of stairs behind me on the end of his lead. I just wanted to get him inside to safety so headed for the door of our flat. I had just put the key in the door and let Bob in when I heard a loud groan. I turned round and saw the guy collapse. He just suddenly went down like a sack of potatoes, hitting the ground with a smack.

'Mate, are you all right?' I said, running over to him. He clearly wasn't.

I could see immediately that he was in a really bad way. He didn't seem to be breathing.

'Oh God, he's OD'd!' I said to myself, recognising the symptoms of an overdose.

Fortunately, I had my cheap Nokia mobile on me. I called 999 and asked for an emergency ambulance. The lady on the other end of the line took my address but then told me it was going to take at least ten minutes.

'Can you describe his condition to me?' she asked, her voice calm and professional.

'He's unconscious and he's not breathing,' I said. 'And his skin is changing colour.'

'OK, sounds like his heart has stopped. I'm going to ask you to give him CPR. Do you know what that is?' the lady said.

'Yes, I do. But you will have to talk me through it really carefully.'

She got me to turn the guy on his side and to check that his airwaves were clear. I then had to turn him on to his back so that I could apply compression to his chest to try to jump start his heart. Then I had to breathe into his mouth to try to get him to respond.

Within moments I was pressing down on his chest with both hands, counting as I did so. When I got to thirty I stopped to see if there was any change in his condition.

The lady from the emergency services was still on the line.

'Any response?' she asked.

'No. Nothing. He's not breathing,' I said. 'I'll try again.'

I carried on like this for what must have been several minutes, pressing his chest furiously in short bursts then breathing into his mouth. Looking back on it later, I was surprised at how calm I felt. I realise now that it was one of those situations where the brain goes into a different mode. The emotional reality of what was happening wasn't registering in my mind at all. Instead, I was just focussing on the physical side of things, trying to get this guy to breathe again. Despite my best efforts, however, his condition remained the same.

At one point he started making a gurgling, snoring sound. I'd heard about the 'death rattle' a person makes as they draw their last breath. I didn't want to think it, but I feared that's what I was hearing here.

After what seemed like an age, I heard the buzzer of my door going so ran over to my flat.

'Ambulance service,' a voice said. I hit the buzzer and told them to come up. Thankfully our flaky lift was now working again, so they arrived on the fifth floor within seconds. They threw down their bags and immediately produced a CPR kit with paddles to conduct electric shocks. They then cut open his t-shirt.

'Stand back, Sir,' one of them said. 'We can take it from here.'

For the next five or so minutes they kept working feverishly to get him moving. But his body was lying there, limp and lifeless. By now the shock was kicking in and I was standing by the doorway, shaking.

Eventually, one of the ambulance men slumped over and turned to the other one: 'No. He's gone,' he said. Slowly and really reluctantly they draped a silver blanket over him and put away their gear.

It was as if I had been struck by a lightning bolt. I was absolutely pole-axed. The ambulance guys asked me if I was all right.

'Just need to go inside and sit down for a second I think,' I told them.

Bob had been inside the flat throughout the drama but had now appeared in the doorway, perhaps sensing that I was upset.

'Come on, mate, let's get you inside,' I said, picking him up. For some reason I didn't want him to see the body lying there. He'd seen similar scenes on the streets of central London, but I just felt protective of him.

A few minutes later I got a knock on the door. The police and some paramedics had arrived in the hallway and a young constable was standing in my doorway.

'I gather you were the person who found him and called 999,' he said.

'Yeah,' I said. I'd gathered myself together a little bit by now, but I was still feeling shaken.

'You did the right thing. I don't think there was much more you could have done for him,' the PC said, reassuringly.

I described how I'd found him on the staircase and seen him go down.

'It seemed to affect him really quickly,' I said.

I told them that I was a recovering addict which, I think, allayed any suspicions they might have had about me somehow being involved with this guy. They knew what addicts were like, as indeed did I. At the end of the day all they care about is themselves. They are so selfish would literally sell their own grandmother or watch their girlfriend die. If an addict had discovered another addict who had overdosed in this way they would have done two things; empty the poor sod's pockets of cash, relieve him of any jewellery and then run away – fast. They might call an ambulance but they wouldn't have wanted to get involved.

The policemen also seemed to know about the flats and its dodgy past. They were pretty understanding.

'OK, Mr Bowen, that's all I need for now, it's unlikely we will need a further statement for the inquest, but we will keep your details on file in case we need to speak to you again,' the PC told me.

We chatted for another moment or two. He told me that they had found some ID on the guy and also some medication which had his name and address on it. It turned out he was on day release from a psychiatric ward.

By the time I saw the officer back out into the hallway, the scene had been completely cleared. It was as if nothing had happened. It was as quiet as a grave in the flats. No one else seemed to be around at this time of the day.

In the quiet I suddenly felt myself being

overwhelmed by what I'd just seen. I couldn't hold back my emotions any longer. Back inside the flat, I just burst into floods of tears. I called Belle on my mobile and asked her to come over that night. I needed to talk to someone.

We sat up until well past midnight and drank a few too many beers. I couldn't get the image of the guy collapsing out of my head.

I was in a state of mild shock for days. On one level, I was shaken by the fact that this poor guy had died in that way. He'd spent his final moments on the floor of an anonymous block of flats, in the company of a complete stranger. That wasn't the way life should work. He was someone's son, maybe someone's brother or even someone's father. He should have been with them or his friends. Where were they? Why weren't they looking after him? I also wondered why on earth he had been allowed out of his psychiatric ward for the day if he was that vulnerable?

But, if I was honest, the thing that hit me hardest was the realisation that this could so easily have been me. It might sound silly now, but I remember thinking that it felt a little bit like Scrooge being visited by the ghost of his not-so-distant past.

For the best part of a decade, I had lived like that. I too had been a phantom figure, hiding away in stairwells and alleyways, lost in my heroin addiction. I had no real memory of the details, of course. Large chunks of my life back then were a complete blur. But it was safe to guess that there were probably dozens – maybe hundreds – of occasions when I could have died alone in some anonymous corner of London, far from the parents, relatives and friends from whom I'd cut myself off.

Thinking about it in the wake of this man's death, part of me couldn't actually believe that I'd lived that way. Had I really been reduced to that? Had I really done those things to myself? A part of me couldn't imagine how on earth I'd been able to insert a needle into my flesh, sometimes four times a day. It seemed unreal, except I knew it was reality. I still bore the scars, literally. I only had to look at my arms and legs to see them.

They reminded me of how fragile my situation remained still. An addict is always living on a knife edge. I would always have an addictive personality and some mental health issues that I knew made me prone to destructive behaviour. All it needed was one moment of weakness and I could be on the way down again. It scared me. But it also stiffened my determination to continue that slow descent to earth that my counsellors had talked about. I didn't want to be that anonymous man on the stairs again. I had to keep moving on.

Chapter 6

The Garbage Inspector

We all have our obsessions in life. For Bob, it's packaging.

The assorted collection of boxes, cartons, wrapping papers and plastic bottles which we use during our day-to-day life around the flat, absolutely fascinate him. And some materials fixate him more than others.

Bubble wrap, naturally, is a source of endless entertainment. What child doesn't love popping the bubbles? Bob goes absolutely crazy with excitement whenever I let him play with a sheet of it. I always keep a watchful eye on him. Each time he pops a cell with his paw or mouth, he turns and gives me a look as if to say 'did you hear that?'

Wrapping paper is another fascination. Whenever I unwrap a present for him, he shows more interest in playing with the fancy paper than with the actual toy itself. He is also endlessly obsessed by the crispy, crunchy cellophane used inside cereal packets and by supermarkets to wrap bread. It never ceases to amaze me, but he can spend half an hour rustling a ball of cellophane. Balls of scrunched up aluminium kitchen foil have the same effect.

There is, however, no question about his absolute favourite type of packaging: cardboard boxes. He basically sees every box he comes across as a toy, an object designed to provide him with hours of fun. If I ever walk past Bob with a cardboard box in my hand he lunges at me as if to grab it. It doesn't matter whether it is a cereal box, a milk carton or a bigger box, he bounds up, paddling his paws quickly as if to say 'give me that, I want to play with it NOW'.

He also loves hiding away in the bigger boxes, a habit that has given me a case of the heebeegeebees on at least one occasion.

I don't let Bob wander out of our flat on his own and the windows are always closed to avoid him climbing out. (I knew cats had the ability to 'self-right' themselves in the air and we were 'only' five floors up, but I didn't want to test his flying abilities!) So when, one summer evening, I couldn't find him in any of his usual spots I panicked slightly.

'Bob, Bob, where are you mate?' I said.

I looked high and low, a process that didn't take too long given the smallness of my flat. But there was no sign of him in my bedroom or in the kitchen or bathroom. I was beginning to genuinely worry about his welfare when it suddenly struck me that I'd put a box containing some hand-me-down clothes I'd been given by a charity worker in the airing cupboard. Sure enough, I opened the cupboard to see a distinctive ginger shape submerged in the middle of the box.

He'd done the same thing again not long afterwards, with almost disastrous consequences.

Belle had come around to help me tidy the place up a bit. It wasn't the most organised and orderly of homes, at the best of times. It didn't help that, for years I had been a bit of a magpie. I don't know whether I subconsciously harboured dreams of opening a junk shop or whether I was just fascinated by old stuff, but somehow I'd collected all sorts of bits and bobs, everything from old books and maps, to broken radios and toasters.

Belle had persuaded me to chuck out some of this old tat and we'd organised a few cardboard boxes full of them. We were going to throw some in the rubbish but take others to charity shops or the local recycling place. Belle was taking one box down to the rubbish area outside the flats and was waiting for the lift to arrive when she felt her box jiggling around. It freaked her out a bit and I heard her scream from inside my flat. By the time I opened the door to see what the trouble was she'd dropped the box to the floor and discovered Bob inside. He was extricating himself from a collection of old books and magazines where he'd curled up for a nap.

Soon after that I'd actually made him a bed out of a cardboard box. I'd figured that if he slept in one he might be less obsessed with them at other times. I'd taken one side off a box then lined it with a little blanket. He was as snug as a bug in there. He loved it.

It didn't entirely get rid of his obsession, however. He remained deeply interested in the rubbish bin in the kitchen. Whenever I put something into the bin he would get up on his hind legs and stick his nose in. If I ever challenged him he would throw me a look as if to say 'hey, what are you throwing in there? I haven't decided if I want to play with that or not.' For a while, I started jokingly calling him the garbage inspector. It wasn't always a laughing matter, however.

I was just emerging from the bath one morning when I heard weird noises coming from the kitchen. I could make out a thin, metallic, scraping sound, as if something was being dragged around. It was accompanied by a kind of low moaning sound.

'Bob, what are you up to now?' I said, grabbing a towel to dry my hair as I went to investigate.

I couldn't help giggling at the sight that greeted me.

Bob was standing in the middle of the kitchen floor with an empty tin of cat food wedged on the top of his head. The tin was sitting at a jaunty angle on his head right over his eyeline. He looked like a cross between the Black Knight from the movie *Monty Python and the Holy Grail* and a Welsh guard outside Buckingham Palace with his bearskin hat hanging over his eyes.

It was obvious that he couldn't see much because he was walking backwards across the kitchen floor, dragging the tin with him in an attempt to reverse himself out of it. He was being very deliberate, padding backwards one careful step at a time, occasionally wiggling the tin or raising it a little before giving it a tap against the floor in the hope the impact would dislodge it. His plan wasn't working. It was comical to watch.

It didn't take Hercule Poirot or Columbo to work out what had happened. In the corner of the room I could see the black bin liner containing the rubbish I was going to put in the wheelie bins downstairs this morning. I normally emptied the bin and put the sack out at night, specifically to stop Bob playing with it. But for some reason today I'd forgotten and left it on the kitchen floor. Big mistake.

Bob had clearly taken advantage of my absence and ripped and chewed at the bottom of the bag so that he could try his luck rummaging in the waste. He'd drawn a blank on the cardboard front, but he had found the old tin. Unfortunately for him, in his enthusiasm to explore its contents, he'd got his head stuck in there. It was the kind of thing you saw on YouTube or video clip programmes like *You've Been Framed* all the time. He'd got himself in a terrible mess and was letting out this rather sad and pathetic little moaning sound. It wasn't the first time he'd done something like this. One day I'd been sitting in the living room when I heard another odd sound coming from the kitchen, a kind of tapping sound. *Pat . . . pat . . . pat* followed by a faster *pat, pat, pat, pat*.

I'd found Bob walking around with a miniature container of butter attached to one of his paws. He loved butter so had obviously found this and been dipping his paw in so that he could lick it clean. He'd somehow wedged the paw inside the container and was now walking around with it attached. Every now and again, he'd raise his paw and tap it against a cupboard door in an effort to dislodge it. Eventually I'd had to help him remove it. I could see I would have to do the same thing here.

He was clearly feeling a little bit sorry for himself and knew he'd done something stupid.

'Bob, you silly boy. What have you done to

yourself?' I said, leaning down to help him. Thank goodness he hadn't shoved his head all the way inside the tin, I thought. It had a serrated edge where it had been opened so I was careful in removing it from his head. I smelled inside the tin. It wasn't the most pleasant odour I'd ever encountered, that was for sure.

The instant I extricated the top of his head from the tin, Bob scooted off into the corner. There were bits of food stuck to his ear and the back of his head so he began licking and washing himself frantically. As he did so he kept shooting me rather sheepish looks, as if to say: 'yes, I know it was a dumb thing to do. Don't tell me you've never done anything stupid yourself.'

As we headed off into work an hour or so later, he was still wearing the same, rather embarrassed expression and I was still smiling to myself about it.

The first sign that something was amiss came a few days later when he began eating more than usual. Bob's daily diet had been a well-established routine for a long time now. Even though money was tight, I always tried to feed him decent 'Scientific Formula' food from the most popular cat food brands. I'd ration it carefully, following the recommended portions. So in the morning he had a flat tea cup full of high-nutrition biscuits and at the end of the day, about an hour before his bed time, he'd then have a further half a tea cup of biscuits along with half a pouch of meat as his evening meal.

These two meals would be supplemented by the little snacks he had while we were out working. It was always more than sufficient to keep him happy and healthy. In fact, he normally left a quarter or so of his morning biscuits because it was too much for him. Sometimes he'd leave it there, at other times he'd eat it just before we headed out to work, as a mid-morning snack.

A few days after he'd got his head caught in the tin can, however, I noticed that he was wolfing down all his breakfast in double-quick time. He was even licking the bowl clean.

He was also more demanding. I had always decided when to give him a reward for his tricks. But now he began to ask for snacks himself. There was something different about the way he pleaded for these snacks as well. It wasn't the usual plaintive, 'Puss in Boots' look. It was as if he was really desperate for food. And it was the same when we got home. Ordinarily, he was pretty laid back about getting his dinner, but he began to hassle me as soon as we were in the door. He would be quite agitated until I filled his bowl up. Again, he'd shovel everything down him as fast as possible and give me a look straight out of *Oliver Twist*. 'Please, dad, can I have some more?'

The alarming thing, however, was that after a week or so of this behaviour he wasn't gaining any weight.

That's odd, I said to myself one evening when he'd finished his dinner and still looked like he could have eaten more.

Adding to my suspicions that something was wrong was the fact that he was going to the toilet more often. Bob was, like most cats, a creature of habit when it came to toilet time. Over the years he'd overcome his dislike of going in the litter tray at home and did his business there in the mornings. He'd then go again when we were out in London. Suddenly, however, this habit had changed and he had started going three times or more each day. He might have been going more than that, as far as I knew. I'd caught him using the toilet in the flat once. I hadn't seen him use it again since then, for some reason. Maybe he didn't like me watching him? But as I began to worry more and more about this change in his habits I noticed the water in the toilet bowl was a little off colour sometimes.

He had also started demanding to be taken to the toilet more often at Angel. It was always a real palaver, packing up and heading over to the Green so that he could get on with things, but it had to be done.

'What is wrong with you, Bob?' I said, losing patience with him after a few days of this. He just gave me an aloof look, as if to tell me to mind my own business.

The moment I knew I had a real problem, however, was when I found him dragging his bottom along the floor. The first time I noticed it was one morning soon after I'd woken up. I saw him deep in concentration, scooting his undercarriage on the carpet in the living room.

I wasn't best pleased.

'Bob, that's disgusting, what do you think you're doing?' I scalded him.

But I soon realised that it must mean that he had a problem. As usual, I was short of money and didn't want to splash out on a visit to the vet and the inevitable medicine expenses that would follow. So the next morning on the way into work I decided to drop into the local library and have a little root around on the internet. I had my suspicions but had to be sure. My hunch was that he had some kind of stomach infection involving a parasite. It didn't necessarily explain the eating, but it was consistent with going to the toilet more often and scooting his bottom on the floor.

My greatest fear was that it was a parasite infection. I cast my mind back to my childhood in Australia when I'd seen a couple of cats develop worms. It wasn't pleasant, and was also contagious. A lot of children in Australia used to contract worms from their cats. It was quite gross actually.

Of course, researching illness on the internet is always the biggest mistake you can make. I'd done it before, but hadn't heeded the lesson. Sure enough, within about half an hour I'd convinced myself that Bob's symptoms were consistent with a really serious kind of worm, a hookworm or a tapeworm. Neither is usually a fatal illness, but they can be really nasty, causing severe loss of weight and a deterioration in the coat if untreated.

I knew I had no option but to check his poo the next time he went to the toilet. I didn't have to wait long. Within about an hour of us settling down at Angel, he started making his tell-tale noises and gestures and I had to take him off to the Green. I braced myself to sneak a quick look before he covered up his business in the soft earth. He didn't take kindly to my intrusion.

'Sorry, Bob, but I've got to take a peek,' I said, inspecting his droppings with a twig.

It may sound bizarre, but I was delighted when I saw some tiny, white wiggly creatures in there. It was worms, but only tiny little ones.

'At least it's not tapeworm or hookworm,' I consoled myself for the rest of that day.

Heading home that night I felt a strange, slightly confusing mix of emotions. The responsible cat owner in me was really miffed. I was so careful about his diet, avoiding raw meats and other things that are known to be risky when it comes to worms.

I had also been diligent in making sure he was regularly checked for fleas, which can act as hosts for worms. He was also a really clean and healthy cat, and I made sure the flat was in a decent condition for him to live. I felt like it reflected badly on me. I felt like I'd let him down a little bit. On the other hand, however, I was relieved that I now knew what I needed to do.

As luck would have it, I knew the Blue Cross drop-in van was going to be at Islington Green the following day. So I made sure that we headed off early to beat the lengthy queues that always built up before the clinic began.

The staff there knew Bob and I well; we'd been regular visitors over the years. Bob had been micro-chipped there and I'd spent the best part of a year dropping in to slowly pay off the fees I'd incurred for that and other treatments. I'd also had him checked out frequently, including for fleas, ironically.

The vet who was on duty that morning asked me to describe the problem, then took a quick look at Bob and a sample of poo that I'd put in a plastic, pill container I had lying around the house before coming to a predictable conclusion.

'Yes, he's got worms I'm afraid, James,' he said. 'What's he been eating lately? Anything out of the ordinary? Been rummaging in the bins or anything like that?'

It was as if a light had gone on in my head. I felt so stupid.

'Oh, God, yes.'

I'd completely forgotten about the tin can incident. He must have found a piece of old chicken or other meat in there. How could I have failed to see that?

The vet gave me a course of medication and a syringe with which to apply it.

'How long will it take to clear things up?' I asked.

'Should be on the mend within a few days, James,' he said. 'Let me know if the symptoms persist.'

Years earlier, when I'd first taken Bob in and had to administer antibiotics to him I'd had to do it by hand, inserting tablets in his mouth and then rubbing his throat to help them on their way down into his stomach. The syringe would, in theory, make that process simpler. But he still had to trust me to insert the contraption down his throat.

Back at the flat that evening, I could tell that he didn't like the look of it. But it was a measure of how much he trusted me that he immediately let me place the plastic inside his mouth and release the tablet before rubbing his throat. I figured that he must know I wouldn't do anything to him that wasn't absolutely necessary.

As the vet had predicted, Bob was back to his normal self within a couple of days. His appetite waned and he was soon eating and going to the toilet normally again.

As I thought about what had happened, I gave myself a ticking off. The responsibility of looking after Bob had been such a positive force in my life. But I needed to live up to that responsibility a little better. He wasn't a part time job that I could clock into whenever the mood took me.

I felt particularly negligent because it wasn't the first time Bob had suffered because of his habit of rummaging in bins. A year or so earlier, he'd got quite sick after investigating the inside of the wheelie bins outside the block of flats.

I told myself that I could never let a bin bag lie around like that again. It was stupid of me to have done so in the first place. Even if everything was sealed, Bob was such a resourceful and inquisitive character, he'd find a way in.

Most of all though, I breathed a sigh of relief. It wasn't often that he was off colour or ill, but whenever he was, the pessimist in me always jumped to the worst possible conclusions. As daft and over-dramatic as it was, over the past days I'd found myself imagining him dying and me having to carry on life without him. It was a prospect that was too scary to contemplate.

I always said that we were partners, that we needed each other equally. Deep down I believed that wasn't really true. I felt like I needed him more.

Chapter 7

Cat on a Hoxton Roof

Bob and I have always been a fairly distinctive pair. There aren't many six foot tall blokes walking around the streets of London with a ginger cat sitting on his shoulders, after all. We certainly turn heads.

For a few months during the summer and autumn of 2009 we made an even more eye-catching sight. Unfortunately, I was in too much pain to enjoy the attention.

The problems had begun the previous year when I'd travelled to Australia to see my mother. My mum and I had always had a difficult relationship and we'd become estranged for the best part of a decade. Apart from a brief visit to London, the last time I'd seen her was when she'd seen me off at the airport as an 18-year-old heading from Australia to 'make it' as a musician in London. In the lost decade that followed, we'd barely talked. Time had healed the wounds a little, so, when she offered to pay for me to visit her in Tasmania, it seemed right that I should go.

With Bob's help I'd just managed to make a massive breakthrough and wean myself off methadone. It had left me feeling weak so I needed the break. Bob had stayed with my friend Belle, at her flat near Hoxton in north London, not too far from Angel.

The long flights to and from Australia had taken their toll on me physically, however. I had known about the risks of spending hours immobile on long haul flights, especially when you are tall, like me, and had done my best to avoid sitting for too long in a cramped seating position. But despite doing my best to walk around the plane as often as possible, I'd come home with a nagging pain in my upper thigh.

At first it had been manageable and I'd dealt with it by taking ordinary, over-the-counter pain killers. Slowly but surely, however, it had grown worse. I had begun experiencing an incredible cramping feeling, as if my blood had stopped flowing and my muscles were seizing up. I know no human feels rigor mortis, but I had a suspicion if we did, this was the sensation. It was as if I had the leg of a zombie.

The pain had soon become so bad that I couldn't sit or lie down with my leg in anything resembling a normal position. If I did I would be in constant muscular pain. So whenever I was watching television or eating a meal at home in the flat I had to sit with my leg on a cushion or another chair. When it came to bedtime I had to sleep with my foot elevated over the end of the bed head.

I'd been to see the doctor a couple of times, but they had only prescribed stronger pain killers. During the dark days of my heroin addiction, I had injected myself everywhere in my body, including in my groin. I'm sure they felt that my condition, whatever it was, was just some kind of hangover from my abusive past. I hadn't pushed it, part of me was used to being fobbed off still. It reinforced that old feeling I'd had as a homeless person that I was somehow invisible, that society didn't regard me as its concern.

The real problem for me was that I still needed to earn a crust. So that meant that, regardless of how much discomfort I was in, I still had to haul myself out of bed and head to Angel on a daily basis.

It wasn't easy. The moment I put my foot on the floor, the pain shot up through my leg like an electric shock. I could only walk three or four steps at a time. So the walk to the bus stop became a marathon, often taking me twice or three times as long as it would normally.

Bob didn't know what to make of this at first. He kept giving me quizzical looks, as if to say: 'what are you doing, mate?' But he was a smart boy and had soon worked out there was something wrong and started changing his behaviour accordingly. In the morning, for instance, rather than greeting me with his usual repertoire of sounds, nudges and pleading looks, he had started looking at me with an inquisitive and slightly pitying expression. It was as if he was saying 'feeling any better today?'

It was the same story as we headed to work. Often Bob would walk alongside me rather than taking up his usual position on my shoulders. He obviously preferred travelling on the upper deck, as I put it, but he would trot along beside me as much as he possibly could. I think he could see I was in pain.

When he felt that I had been soldiering on for too long he would actually try to make me stop and sit down. He would cut across my path, trying to steer me in the direction of a bench or wall where I could take a break. I took the view that it was better to finish my journey rather than stopping every few steps so, for a while, it developed into a bit of a battle of wills.

It must have been quite entertaining when locals in Tottenham saw us picking our way down the road near my flats. Whenever he heard me complain about the pain Bob would stop and give me a look that suggested I should take a breather or sit down. I'd look back at him and say, 'No, Bob, I need to keep moving.' If I hadn't been in so much agony, I'd probably have found it quite amusing myself. We probably resembled a bickering old married couple.

After a while, however, it became pretty clear that I couldn't carry on like this. Often I'd arrive home from work exhausted, only to discover that the lift was out of order again. The walk to the fifth floor was absolutely excruciating and could take an eternity. So I had begun staying with Belle.

There were all sorts of advantages to this. To begin with her flat was on the first floor rather than the fifth floor which saved me a lot of aggravation. Getting to work from there was also a less painful process with a bus stop only yards away.

It helped a little, but the pain continued to grow gradually worse. My dread of putting my foot on the floor had now become so great that one morning I decided to make myself a crutch. With Bob in tow, I'd headed into the pretty little park near Belle's flat and found a branch from a fallen tree that fitted perfectly under my arm, allowing me to keep the weight off my painful leg when I walked. It only took me a day or so to get the hang of it.

I got a lot of very strange looks, understandably. With my long hair and shaggy beard, I must have looked like some kind of modern-day Merlin or Gandalf from *The Lord of the Rings*. As if that wasn't odd enough, the sight of a ginger cat sitting on my shoulder must have conjured up images of wizards walking around with their 'familiars'. The truth was that I didn't really care what it looked like at that point. Anything that eased the pain was a Godsend.

Getting anywhere on foot had become a real ordeal. I was taking a few steps and then keeling over and sitting on the nearest brick wall. I'd tried using the bike to get around but that was an utter impossibility. The moment I applied any pressure to the pedal with my right leg I was in agony. The Bobmobile was in the hallway back in Tottenham, gathering dust.

There was no question that Bob understood that there was something seriously wrong with me and at times I felt like he was losing patience. Some mornings, as he watched me struggling to get my trousers on ready to go to work, he would give me a withering look as if to say: 'why are you doing this to yourself? Why don't you stay in bed?' The answer to that, of course, was that I had no option. We were skint, as usual.

My daily routine became a real chore. We'd get off the bus at Islington Green and head to the little park there so that Bob could do his business. From there, I'd hobble over to the *The Big Issue* co-ordinator's spot, which was just outside Starbucks coffee shop. I'd then cross the main road and head to the tube station, and our pitch.

Having to stand there for five or six hours a day wasn't feasible. I would have passed out. Fortunately, one of the florists outside the tube station saw the state I was in one day and came over to me holding a couple of buckets that he used to hold flowers.

'There you go, sit on that. And get Bob to sit on the other one,' he had said, giving me an encouraging pat on the back.

I really appreciated it. There was no way I was going to be able to stand for more than a few minutes at a time.

At first, I'd been worried that sitting on the bucket would be a disaster for my business. (People always laughed when I called selling *The Big Issue* a business, but that's actually what it was. You had to buy magazines in order to sell them so, as a vendor, you had to make fine judgements about stock and budgeting week in, week out. The principle was actually no different from running a giant corporation and the stakes were just as high, if not higher. Succeed and you survived, fail and you could starve to death.) Ordinarily, I paced around the area outside the station coaxing and cajoling people into parting with their hard-earned cash. When I started sitting on the bucket, I was terrified that people simply wouldn't see me sitting there. I should have known better. Bob took care of it.

Maybe it was because I was sitting down with him more of the time, but during this period he became a real little showman. In the past, it had usually been me who had instigated the playful routines. But now he began taking the initiative himself. He would rub up against me and give me a look as if to say, 'come on mate, get the snacks out, let's do a few tricks and earn ourselves a few quid'. There were times when I was convinced he knew precisely what was happening. I was certain he'd worked out that the sooner we earned a decent amount of money, the sooner we could get home and rest my leg. It was eerie how he understood so much.

I wished I could see life so clearly sometimes.

Living at Belle's with Bob had its pros and cons. I was still desperately trying to work out what was wrong with my leg, but just hoped that by resting it the problem would somehow go away. While I spent as much time as I could off my feet, Belle looked after me, cooking me nice meals and doing my laundry, and Bob got on well with her. During the time he'd spent with her while I was in Australia, they had clearly formed a strong bond. She was the only other person whom he would ever consider allowing to pick him up, for instance.

There was no doubt that he regarded her home as a safe haven as well. The previous year, when he'd run away from Angel one evening after being attacked by a dog, he'd headed for Belle's flat, even though it had been a long walk away. It had taken me hours to work out that he'd taken refuge there. It had been the longest night of my life.

The closeness of their relationship certainly made life easier for me. But it also gave Bob licence to be mischievous.

One morning I got up and headed into the kitchen to make myself a cup of coffee, expecting to find Bob settled there. Just like at home, he tended to hang around in the kitchen early in the day, mainly in the hope of picking up any spare bits of food that might be going. There were times when he could be a real gannet.

Today, however, there was no sign of him. There was no sign of Belle either.

It had been raining heavily that morning but the weather had already cleared. It was now a really bright sunny morning and the temperature was already rising. The forecast was predicting sweltering heat later in the day. I noticed that Belle had already opened the window in the kitchen to let the fresh air into the flat.

'Bob, where are you mate?' I said, heading off in search of him, still wearing just my boxer shorts and a t-shirt.

There was no sign of him in the sitting room or the hallway, so I headed to the back bedroom where Belle slept. When I saw the window there was also ajar I got an instant sinking feeling.

Belle's flat was on the first floor and the back bedroom window overlooked the roof of the extension on the ground floor flat below us. That roof overlooked a yard and, beyond it, the car park for the building. From there it was a short walk to the main road, one of the busiest in that part of north London.

'Oh, no, Bob, you haven't gone out there have you?'

I managed to squeeze my head through the gap in the window and scanned the rooftops below. There were extension roofs protruding all the way along the building. Sure enough, five flats along from Belle's, there was Bob sitting, sunning himself on the roof.

When I shouted his name he slowly turned his head in my direction and gave me a confused look. It was as if he was saying: 'what's wrong?'

I had no problem with him sunbathing. I was more concerned with the fact that he could slide off the slippery roof, or that he might go down into the yard and from there out through the car park on to the main road.

I panicked and began taking the security screws off the window so that I could open it fully and climb out on to the roof. After a couple of minutes I was able to squeeze myself through the gap. I still hadn't managed to put on any clothes.

The slate tiles were slippery from the rain earlier in the morning, so keeping a grip wasn't easy, especially given the fact I was in agony with my leg. Somehow, however, I managed to scamper across the rooftops to where Bob was sitting. I was within a few feet of him when I realised that I was on a wasted mission.

Bob suddenly picked himself up and scuttled his way back across the rooftops, nonchalantly passing me. When I tried to grab at him, he just growled at me and made a sudden spurt towards Belle's open window. Again, he shot me a disdainful look. He was soon disappearing back indoors.

I, of course, had a long way to go. It took me a few minutes to scramble back across the slippery slates. To my complete embarrassment, a couple of faces appeared in the windows. The looks on their faces spoke volumes. They were a mix of shock, mild pity and hilarity.

Moments after I got back into the safety of the flat, I heard the front door closing and saw Belle standing in the hallway with a small bag of groceries.

She burst out laughing.

'Where the hell have you been?' she said.

'On the bloody roof trying to rescue Bob,' I said.

'Oh he goes out there all the time,' she said with a dismissive wave of a hand. 'He even goes down into the yard sometimes. He always comes back up.'

'I really wish you'd told me that sooner,' I said, shuffling off to my temporary bedroom to finally put on some clothes.

It wasn't long before he'd turned the tables, however. Soon after that, it was Belle who was cursing his playful ways.

As I'd discovered the hard way, Bob loved exploring the back of Belle's block of flats and took full advantage of the fact that he was on the first rather than the fifth floor.

In some ways it was a healthy thing. Bob loved going out there to do his business in the mornings and evenings. But, of course, this also allowed him to exercise his other natural instincts.

I knew that it was part of his DNA to hunt. No matter how much people might think they are cute little fluffballs, cats are also predators – seriously effective predators at that. As we settled into life at Belle's flat, he began to bring us presents. One day we were sitting in the front room when he arrived with a small mouse dangling from his mouth. He'd placed it carefully at my feet, as if he was offering me a gift.

I'd chastised him about it.

'Bob, you will make yourself sick again if you eat that,' I said.

Realistically I knew there was nothing I could do, apart from keeping him under house arrest, which I didn't want to do. And I wasn't going to resort to putting a bell on him, at this stage, at least.

Predictably, this meant that he became a little bolder in his behaviour.

One morning, I was lying on my bed, reading, when I heard the most almighty scream. It was Belle.

'Oh, my God, oh my God.'

I jumped up and ran into the living room where she was doing some ironing. There, sitting on top of a pile of freshly-pressed shirts and bed sheets, was a little brown frog.

'James, James, pick it up, get rid of it. Please,' she said, calming down slightly.

I noticed Bob standing in the doorway taking all this in. There was a strange expression on his face, what I could only call mischievousness. It was as if he knew exactly what had happened.

I got hold of the little frog and cupped it in my hands. I then walked the long way round via the front door to the area at the back of the building with Bob following me every step of the way.

I went back inside, started to read my book and forgot all about it. But then, about an hour or so later, I heard another scream, accompanied by the sound of something hitting a wall. This time it was coming from the hallway.

'What is it now?' I said, heading towards the kerfuffle.

Belle was standing at one end of the corridor with her hands on her head and a horrified expression on her face. She pointed down the corridor at a pair of slippers that she'd clearly thrown down the hallway.

'It's inside my slipper now,' she said.

'What's inside your slipper?' I said, puzzled.

'The frog.'

I had to suppress a laugh. But, again, I retrieved the frog and took it out to the garden. Again Bob marched behind me, trying to look like it was a pure coincidence that this frog had now appeared inside the flat twice in the space of an hour or so.

'Stay there, mate,' I said, sensing that I had to make sure I disposed of the frog properly this time.

He looked at me disapprovingly then turned and slinked off back into the house as if to say, 'you're really no fun at all!'

🐾

As comfortable as we were at Belle's, after a while I began to realise that it wasn't ideal, in particular for my relationship with Bob.

The pain in my leg had made me short-tempered and generally less fun to be around than usual. So, perhaps inevitably, as time wore on, Bob and I had started spending less and less time together. Sensing that I was sleeping longer and wasn't in the best of moods when I woke up, he wouldn't always come into the bedroom for an early morning play. Often Belle would rustle up a breakfast for him instead. He would also head off out of the window to explore the back of the flats on a regular basis and would sometimes be gone for long stretches. I imagined he must be having a great time out there.

I also had a very strong suspicion that he was eating elsewhere too. He had begun arriving home from his sessions out on the roof and in the yard around supper time. But when Belle or I put down a bowl for him, he did little more than play with his food. At first my heart sank a little. *He's eating in the bins again*, I said to myself. But Belle and I checked the garbage area at the back of the building and came to the conclusion there was no way he could get into the giant, locked receptacles. The explanation must lay elsewhere.

One day, when we were heading out to work, I saw an elderly gentleman downstairs, collecting his mail. Bob saw him and fixed him with a knowing stare.

'Hello young fellow,' the man said. 'Nice to see you again.'

Suddenly it made sense. I remembered that children's book *Six Dinner Sid* by Inga Moore, about a cat that charms its way into the affections of everyone on his street, earning himself a dinner in every house each night. Bob had pulled the same stunt. He had become Six Dinner Bob.

In a way it was a sign of how comfortable and happy he was making himself there. But it was also a sign that he was getting used to life without me at the centre of his world. Lying there at night, trying to think about anything and everything but the throbbing pain in my leg, I began to ask myself something I'd not asked in all the time we'd been together. Would he be better off without me?

It was a fair question. Who needed to be hanging around with a crippled, ex-junkie with no money and no job prospects? Who needed to be out on the streets in all kinds of weather being poked and prodded by passers-by? Especially when there were friendlier, less complicated souls around to give you a square meal every day.

I'd always felt that I could give Bob as good a life as anyone else, if not a better one. We were soul mates, two chips off the same block, I told myself. For the first time since we'd got together, I wasn't so sure about that any more.

Chapter 8

None So Blind

It's incredible what pain does to the human mind. At night in particular, you lie there, unable to sleep, hallucinating, thinking the most insane things. At one point, for instance, I began to fantasise about having my leg amputated. I imagined having a prosthetic limb instead of the throbbing, bloated one I now had – and was actually comforted by the thought.

Another time, I was limping through the car park in a local supermarket when I saw a wheelchair, sitting there unoccupied. A man was lowering a hydraulic ramp on the back of a small van, from where, I assumed, the chair's owner would soon be helped out. The thought of being able to travel around without having to put any weight on my foot was really tempting. For a split second, I thought about stealing it. I was ashamed of myself the moment the idea entered my head.

As I lay there in a kind of fever some nights, I

also found myself thinking more and more about Bob, or more specifically, losing Bob. The worse my leg became, the more I became convinced that he was ready to leave. I imagined him in the company of the old man next door, being pampered and fussed over. I pictured him lying on the sunny roof at Belle's without a worry in the world while I hobbled off to sell *The Big Issue* on my own.

It wasn't such a leap of the imagination. Back at Belle's I was spending more and more time on my own, lying in my room asleep. As a result, I had less patience for Bob than usual. He'd sidle up to me on the bed, waiting to play catch with some treats, but I'd fail to respond. Sometimes he would try to drape himself around my leg, which I found unbearable. By now my leg was a violent, red colour and the pain was relentless.

'Go away and play somewhere else, Bob,' I'd say, brushing him to one side. He'd reluctantly slide off me and head out of the bedroom door, throwing me a disappointed look as he went. It was hardly a surprise that he was starting to look elsewhere for affection, I told myself afterwards.

I'm not much of a friend to him at the moment.

I knew it wasn't helping anyone, least of all myself, but I didn't know what to do to dig myself out of the black hole that had been slowly consuming me these past few weeks. One morning, however, I woke up and decided that enough was enough. I simply had to do something about it. I didn't care what the doctors thought about me and my past: I wanted some answers, I wanted this problem to go away. I got dressed, grabbed my crutch and headed for the local surgery, determined to have a proper examination.

'That's an interesting crutch you have there, Mr Bowen,' the doctor said when I turned up in the consulting room.

'Necessity is the mother of invention,' I said, sticking the weather-beaten pole in the corner and climbing on to the examination table where he began casting an eye over my thigh and leg.

'This doesn't look too good. You need to keep pressure off that leg for a week or so. Can you take time off work?' he asked me.

'No, not really. I sell *The Big Issue*,' I told him.

'OK, well you need to see what you can do to keep your foot elevated at all times,' he said. 'I also need you to have what's known as a D-Dimer blood test which looks for clotting in the blood cells. I suspect that's where your problems lie.'

'OK,' I said.

'Now, what are we going to do about this crutch

of yours? I think we can do better than a tree branch,' he said.

'No chance of a wheelchair?' I said, suddenly remembering the one I'd seen in the car park.

'Afraid not. But I could offer you a decent set of crutches while we try to get this swelling and inflammation down.'

By the end of the morning I was the proud owner of a pair of proper metallic crutches, complete with rubber grips, arm holders and shock absorbers. I was soon clunking my way around with my legs flailing in front of me. I was acutely conscious of the way it must have looked. I felt silly, even sillier than I'd looked with a pole under my arm. I could feel what people were thinking about me. It was depressing.

The time for feeling sorry for myself was over, however. I didn't waste any time and went to have the blood test done the following day. It wasn't that straightforward, of course. Taking a blood sample from a recovering heroin addict is easier said than done.

The practice nurse at the clinic asked me to roll up my sleeve but when she tried to find a vein she failed miserably.

'Hmmm, let's try this other arm instead,' she said. But it was the same again.

We exchanged a look that spoke volumes. I didn't need to spell it out.

'Maybe I should do it,' I said.

She gave me a sympathetic look and handed me the needle. Once I'd found a vein in my leg, I let her extract the sample. The humiliations of being a recovering addict were endless, but I wasn't going to let that deter me.

A couple of days later when I rang the clinic the female doctor confirmed my worst suspicions. She told me that I had developed a deep vein thrombosis, or DVT.

'You have a blood clot which I'd like to have further investigated. So I need you to go to University College Hospital for an ultrasound test,' she told me.

In a way it was a relief. I'd always suspected I'd caused myself a problem on those long flights to and from Australia. Looking back on it I could see that I'd suppressed the thought for all sorts of silly reasons, partly because I hadn't wanted to sound paranoid but partly also because I hadn't wanted to have my suspicions confirmed. I knew that DVTs could cause all sorts of problems, particularly coronary ones, strokes in particular.

Given all this, I was on edge over the next week or so while I waited for the ultrasound appointment. Bob and I carried on going to work but I was only going through the motions. I was terrified to do something that might trigger a stroke or heart attack. I even stopped interacting with him when we sat on the buckets together. He'd look at me every now and again, expecting me to produce a treat so that we could start performing for the commuters. But more often than not my heart wasn't in it and I'd turn away. Looking back, I was too wrapped up in myself. If I'd looked I'm sure I'd have seen the disappointment written all over his face.

When the appointment day came I dragged myself to UCH on the Euston Road and passed through a room of expectant mothers waiting in the ultra-sound department. I seemed to be the only person who wasn't excited to be there.

I was led off by a specialist who slapped loads of jelly on my leg so that he could run the camera around, the same as they did for the mums-to-be. It turned out that I had a massive, six-inch-long blood clot. The specialist sat me down and told me that he suspected it had started as a small clot but had thickened and clotted further along the edge of the vein.

'It was probably hot weather that set it off and then you've exacerbated it by walking around on it,' he said. 'We will prescribe you a blood thinning medicine and that should sort it out.'

I was relieved. Unfortunately, I wasn't quite in the clear.

I was prescribed an anti-coagulant that is used a lot to thin the blood of potential stroke victims. But I didn't pay any attention to the leaflet that came with it. It didn't occur to me that there might be side effects.

A few nights after I started taking the tablets, I got up at around 5am to go to the toilet. Outside it was pitch black, but there was just about enough light in the flat for me to find my way to the bathroom and back. As I walked down the corridor I could feel something trickling down my thigh. I turned on a light and was horrified to see that my leg was covered in blood. When I got back into my room and switched on the lights, I saw that the sheets of my bed were soaked red as well.

Bob had been fast asleep in the corner, but woke up. He could tell there was something wrong and shot up to stand at my side.

I had no idea what was happening. But I did know that I had to get myself to a hospital – and fast. I threw on a pair of jeans and a jumper and ran out of the flat, heading towards Tottenham High Road where I figured I had a chance of catching a bus.

When I got to UCH, they admitted me immediately. I was told that the anti-coagulant had thinned my blood to such an extent that it had started bleeding from the pores of the weakened skin where I used to inject myself.

I was kept in for two days while they sorted out my medication. They eventually settled on another drug, which wouldn't have the same effect. That was the good news. The bad news was that I'd have to inject it into my stomach myself for a period of up to six months.

Having to inject myself was awful, for all sorts of reasons. To begin with it was painful, injecting directly into my stomach muscles. I could feel the contents of the syringe entering the tissue. Secondly, it was another reminder of my past. I hated the prospect of having a syringe and a needle as part of my daily life once more.

Worst of all, however, it didn't work.

Even after I'd been injecting myself with the new drug for a couple of weeks, my leg was no better. I couldn't walk more than two paces, even with the crutches. I was now beginning to despair. Once again, I began to imagine losing my leg altogether. I went back to UCH and explained the situation to one of the doctors I'd seen previously.

'We'd better have you back in for a week. I'll check to see what the bed situation is right now,' he said, picking up the phone.

I wasn't best pleased about it. It meant I'd not be able to work and I'd already lost two days in hospital. But I knew that I simply couldn't carry on in this condition. I was told that they had a bed the following day. So I went home that night and explained the situation to Belle. She agreed to look after Bob, which was a huge comfort for me. I knew he was happy there. The following morning I got up and packed a small bag of stuff to take to hospital.

I'm not the greatest hospital patient. The clue is in the word *patient*. That's not something I've ever been accused of being. I get easily distracted.

During the first few days, I didn't sleep very well at all, even when they gave me medication to help me nod off. Inevitably, I started taking stock of my life and lay there worrying about everything – my leg, my long term health, my pitch at Angel and, as always, the lack of money. I also lay there and fretted about Bob.

The idea that we should go our separate ways had refused to go away. We'd been together for more than two and a half years now and he had been the most loyal friend imaginable. But all friendships go through phases, and some come to an end. I could see that I'd not been the most brilliant company in recent weeks. Should I ask Belle if she wanted to keep him? Maybe I should ask the nice bloke next door with whom he'd already struck up a bond, it seemed? I would, of course, be devastated to lose him. He was my best friend, my rock. I didn't have anyone else in my life. Deep down I needed him to keep me on the straight and narrow, to maintain my sanity sometimes. But at the same time, I had to make the right choice. I really didn't know what to do. But then it struck me. It wasn't my decision.

As the old saying went, cats choose you, not the other way around. That's what had happened with Bob and me years earlier. For whatever reason, he'd seen something in me that made him want to stick around. I'd always believed in karma, the notion that you get back in life what you put out into the world. Maybe I'd been gifted his company in reward for something good I'd done earlier in life? Not that I could remember doing that much good. Now I had to wait to see if he'd choose me again. If he wanted to remain with me, then it would be his decision. And his alone.

I'd find out his answer soon enough, I felt sure.

When the results of the latest round of tests came in, I was told that the dosage of the drug that had originally been prescribed wasn't strong enough. They were going to increase it, but they also wanted to keep me in longer to make sure it actually had an impact.

'It will only be a couple more days, just to see it

works and doesn't have any side effects,' the doctor told me.

Belle popped in to see me, dropping off a couple of books and some comics. She told me Bob was fine.

'I think he's found someone else to feed him as well as that old guy,' she said, laughing. 'He really is living up to the name Six Dinner Bob.'

After a couple of days it was obvious that the new dosage was finally sorting out my DVT. When I looked at my leg the swelling was beginning to go down and the colour returning to normality. The nurses and doctors could see this as well, so they wasted no time in getting me off my back.

'It's not good for you lying there all day, Mr Bowen,' one of them kept saying to me.

So they insisted that I got out and walked up and down the corridor at least a couple of times a day. It was actually a joy to be able to pace around without wincing with pain. When I put weight on my leg, I didn't get those same excruciating shooting sensations. It still hurt, but it wasn't anywhere near as bad as previously.

True to their word, about a week after I'd been admitted, the doctors told me that I could go home. I texted Belle with the good news. She texted me back to say she'd try to come to the hospital to meet me later that afternoon.

The hospital paperwork took longer than I'd

hoped so it was approaching evening by the time I slipped out of my pyjamas, got dressed, gathered together my belongings and limped my way to the exit on Euston Road. I still had the crutches but didn't really need them. I could now put pressure on my leg without any real pain.

Belle had texted me again to say that she would meet me outside.

'Can't come into hospital. Will explain when I see you,' she'd written.

We'd agreed to meet by the infamous new modern art sculpture outside the main entrance. I'd heard people at the hospital talking about the work of art, a giant, six ton polished pebble. It had cost the hospital tens of thousands of pounds apparently and was meant to make patients and visitors 'feel better' as they arrived and departed. It didn't inspire me particularly, but I certainly felt the benefit of it when my body hit the cold evening air outside. I leaned on it for a moment or two as I tried to catch my breath after walking what seemed like miles along the corridors without the aid of crutches.

I was a couple of minutes early so there was no sign of Belle. That was no surprise at this time of the evening; I could see that the rush hour traffic was already building up. I was resigned to waiting a while, but then, to my relief, I saw her emerging from the bus stop across the road. She was carrying a large, holdall style bag which, I assumed, had some clean clothes and my jacket in it. At first I didn't spot it, but as she got closer I saw a flash of ginger fur poking out of the unzipped top of the bag.

As she reached the bottom of the steps, I saw his head poking out.

'Bob,' I said, excited.

The moment he registered my voice he began scrambling out of the bag. In an instant he had his front paws on Belle's arm and the back ones on the top of the bag, ready to spring forward.

We were still a few feet apart when Bob launched himself off the bag towards me. It was the most athletic leap I'd ever seen him make, and that was saying a lot.

'Whoaah there, fella,' I said, lurching forward to catch him then holding him close to my chest. He pinned himself to me like a limpet clinging on to a rock that was being pounded by waves. He then nuzzled his head in my neck and started rubbing me with his cheeks.

'Hope you don't mind, but that's why I couldn't come in. I had to bring him,' Belle said beaming. 'He saw me packing a few things for you and started going crazy. I think he knew I was coming to get you.'

Whatever doubts I'd had about our future together were swept away in that instant. On the way home, Bob was all over me – literally. Rather than sitting alongside me he sat on my lap, crawled on my shoulders and sat up with his paws on my chest, purring away contentedly.

It was as if he never wanted to let me go again. I felt exactly the same way.

They say that there are none so blind as those who will not see. In the days and weeks that followed, I realised that I had been unwilling, or maybe unable, to see what was glaringly obvious. Far from wanting to leave me, Bob had been desperate to help ease my pain and get me on the road to recovery. He'd given me space to recover. But he'd also been nursing me without my knowledge.

Belle told me that whenever I was asleep in my room, Bob would check up on me. He would lie on my chest and even run checks every now and again.

'He'd give you a little tap on the forehead and wait for you to react. I think he just wanted to make sure you were still with us,' she smiled.

At other times, she told me, he would wrap himself around my leg.

'It was as if he was trying to apply a tourniquet or something. It was like he wanted to take away the pain,' she said. 'You would never lie still long enough for him to stay there for long. But he knew where the pain was and was definitely trying to do something about it.'

I hadn't seen any of this. What was worse, whenever Bob had tried to help or comfort me when I was awake, I'd driven him away. I'd been selfish. Bob loved – and needed – me as much I loved and needed him. I wouldn't forget that.

Lying in bed for days on end had focussed my mind on something else as well. A few weeks after I was back on my feet, I took the most important step I'd made in years. Perhaps in my entire life.

When I'd actually heard the words at a regular appointment with my drug counsellor at the specialist dependency unit in Camden, they'd not sunk in at first.

'I think you've reached the finishing line, James,' he'd said.

'Sorry what do you mean?'

I'm going to write you your final prescription. A few more days of taking your medication and I think you'll be ready to call yourself clean.'

I'd been attending the clinic for several years now. I'd arrived there a mess, addicted to heroin and on a fast track to an early grave. Thanks to a brilliant collection of counsellors and nurses, I'd been hauling myself back from the brink ever since.

After coming off first heroin and then methadone, my new medication, subutex, had slowly but surely been helping me to wean myself off opiates completely. I'd been taking it for around six months now.

They called it a miracle drug and, as far as I was concerned, at least, that's exactly what it was. It had allowed me to reduce my craving for drugs gently and without any hiccups. I'd been reducing my dosage of subutex steadily, first from 8 milligrams to 6 then to 4 and then 2. From there I'd started taking even smaller doses, measured in 0.4 grams. It had been a pretty seamless process, much easier than I'd anticipated.

So I wasn't quite sure why I left the unit that morning feeling so apprehensive about the fact that I was about to stop taking subutex altogether.

I should have been delighted. It was time for that soft aeroplane landing that one of my counsellors had talked about. But I was curiously on edge, and remained that way for the next two days.

That first night, for instance, I started sweating and having minor palpitations. They weren't serious. They were certainly nothing compared to what I'd been through when I'd come off methadone. That had been hellish. It was almost as if I was waiting for something awful to happen, for me to have some dramatic reaction. But nothing happened. I just felt, well, absolutely fine.

Bob was attuned to my mood and sensed that I needed a little more TLC. He wasn't overt; he didn't need to perform any of his late night diagnoses or tap me on the head to check I was still breathing. He just positioned himself a few inches closer on the sofa and gave me an extra rub of his head on my neck every now and again.

I carried on with my life as normal over the next couple of days. Bob and I had headed back to the flat in Tottenham where we'd adjusted to life there again. It was such a relief to be able to walk properly and to ride my bike around with Bob on board.

In the end there was a slight sense of anti-climax. Five or six days after I had been given the final prescription, I pulled the foil container out of its packet and saw that there was just one tablet left.

I squeezed the oval shaped pill out, placed it under my tongue until it had all dissolved then downed a glass of water. I scrunched the foil up into a ball and threw it on the floor for Bob to chase.

'There you go, mate. That's the last one of those you'll get to play with.'

That night, I went to bed expecting to have a rough night. *I will never sleep*, I told myself. I felt sure that my body was going to be racked by withdrawal pangs. I expected nightmares, visions, restless twisting and turning. But there was none of that. There was nothing. Maybe I'd simply exhausted myself with anxiety, but the moment my head hit the pillow I was out like a light.

When I woke up the next morning, I gathered my senses and thought to myself: *Jeez. That's it. I'm clean*. I looked out the window at the London skyline. It wasn't a glorious blue sky, unfortunately. It wasn't quite that clichéd. But it certainly was a clear one. And, just as when I'd come off methadone, it seemed somehow brighter and more colourful.

I knew that the days, weeks, months and years stretching ahead of me weren't going to be easy. There would be times when I would feel stressed, depressed and insecure and at those times I knew that niggling temptation would return and I'd think about taking something to deaden the pain, to kill the senses.

That had been why I'd fallen for heroin in the first place. It had been loneliness and hopelessness that had driven me into its arms. But now I was determined that wasn't going to happen again. Life wasn't perfect, far from it. But it was a million times better than it had been when I'd formed my addiction. Back then I couldn't see beyond the next hit. Now I felt like I could see a way forward. I knew that I could soldier on.

From that day onwards, each time I felt myself weakening I told myself: 'hold on, no, I'm not sleeping rough, I'm not alone, it's not hopeless. I don't need it.'

I carried on seeing a counsellor for a while, but soon I didn't need that either. A month or so after I'd taken my last tablet of subutex he signed me off.

'I don't need to see you again,' he said as he ushered me out of the door. 'Stay in touch, but good luck. And well done.'

And I am happy to say I have not seen or heard from him since.

Chapter 9

Bob's Big Night Out

As we walked south across the Thames at Waterloo Bridge, the lights of the Houses of Parliament and the London Eye were blazing bright in the late November night sky and the pavement was busy with people. Most were heading in the same direction, away from the West End and the City towards the commuter trains of Waterloo station. Some were weary looking office workers, shuffling home from a late night at work, others were in a jollier mood after a night out in the West End.

It was approaching 10.30pm, the end of their day. For me and Bob, on the other hand, it was the beginning of what promised to be a very, very long night.

I'd been persuaded by *The Big Issue* to take part in a new event that they were staging. I had first read about it in the magazine a few months earlier. It was called the 'The Big Night Out' and had been planned to coincide with the 18th birthday of the magazine. With that in mind, some bright spark had decided it would be a good idea to organise an 18 mile walk through the streets of London in the middle of the night.

The idea was that ordinary people could walk through the deserted city between 10pm and 7am with a group of *The Big Issue* vendors so that they could learn a little about the reality of living rough and sleeping on the streets. The adverts in the magazine called it 'a fantastic opportunity to join other like-minded people who have a sense of adventure and a desire to help empower homeless and vulnerable people across the UK'. We hadn't even finished the walk to the start of the event, but I was already beginning to wonder whether it was an adventure too far for me and Bob, especially given the problems I'd had with my leg. It was a bitterly cold night – and getting colder by the minute.

I'd made the decision to take part for a couple of reasons. First and foremost, it was a chance to earn a few extra pounds. Every vendor that took part in the walk was eligible for 25 to 30 free copies of *The Big Issue*. That meant that I could earn about £60 potentially. Beyond that, however, I saw it as an opportunity to talk to people about the magazine and the lives of the people who sold it.

Despite the ups and downs I'd had with the company, I was still a believer in its mission. It was, without question, the salvation for many people who lived on the streets. It had certainly helped give me direction and purpose – not to mention enough money to keep the wolf from the door – along the way.

We were meeting at the IMAX cinema at the Bullring roundabout on the south side of Waterloo Bridge. It was a fitting location. Not so long ago, the roundabout – well, more specifically the labyrinth of concrete, subterranean walkways underneath it – had been home to the shanty town that Londoners knew as Cardboard City. During the 1980s and early 1990s, it had become a home for more than 200 'rough sleepers' as the social workers called us. A lot of those who hung out there were transient junkies and alcoholics but many created homes for themselves from wooden pallets and cardboard boxes. Some even had living rooms and bedrooms with mattresses. It had been a haven, but not necessarily a safe one, for 15 years. I'd stayed there briefly during its final days, at the end of 1997 and early 1998, when everyone was evicted to make way for the IMAX cinema.

My memories of the place were sketchy, but when I walked into the IMAX I saw the organisers of the walk had created a little picture exhibition on the history of Cardboard City. With Bob on my shoulder, I scanned the grainy black and white images for faces that I recognised. As it turned out, I was looking in the wrong place.

'Hello, James,' a female voice said behind me. I recognised it straight away.

'Hello, Billie,' I said.

Back around the year 2000, when my life was at its lowest ebb, Billie and I had become friendly, helping each other out and keeping each other company. We hadn't met until after the demise of Cardboard City and had huddled up against the cold together at the cold-weather shelters that charities like Centrepoint and St Mungo's used to put up during the winter months.

It turned out that Billie had turned her life around too. She'd had an epiphany one night when she was sleeping rough in central London and was disturbed from her sleep by a *Big Issue* seller. At first she'd been annoyed at being woken up by him. She hadn't even known what the magazine was. But she'd looked at it then and grasped the idea. She had then rebuilt her life and, a decade later, was now a 'poster child' for The Big Issue Foundation.

We reminisced about the bad old days over a cup of tea.

'Remember that pop-up at Admiralty Arch during that really snowy winter?' she said.

'Yeah, what year was that? 1999 or 2000 or 2001?' I said.

'Can't remember. Those days are all a blur aren't they?' she said with a resigned shrug.

'Yep. Still, we are here, which is more than can be said for some of the poor sods we were with then.'

Goodness knows how many of the people who had been on the streets with us had perished in the cold or from drugs or violence.

Billie was very committed to this walk.

'It will give people an idea what we had to go through,' she said. 'They won't be able to slip off home into a warm bed, they'll have to stay out there with us.'

I wasn't quite so sure. No one, no matter how well meaning, could really understand what it was like to live on the streets.

Billie, like me, had a companion these days. Hers was a lively Border Collie called Solo. She and Bob weighed each other up for a few minutes but then decided there was nothing to worry about.

Just before 10.30pm John Bird, the founder of *The Big Issue* arrived. I'd encountered him a few times and found him a charismatic character. As usual, he was good value, and fired everyone up with an inspiring little speech about the difference the magazine had made during its 18 years. By now 100 or more people had gathered there along with a couple of dozen vendors, co-ordinators and staff. We all filed out into the night, ready for John Bird to do the countdown.

'Three, two, one,' he shouted and then we were off.

'Here we go, Bob,' I said, making sure he was positioned comfortably on my shoulders.

For me it was a real journey into the unknown. On the one hand, I was really worried about whether my leg would stand up to 18 miles of wear and tear, but on the other I was just delighted to be off my crutches and walking normally again. It was such a relief not to be going 'clonk, clonk, clonk' down the road all the time, having to swing my legs in front of me every step of the way. So, as we set off on the first leg around the South Bank and across the Millennium Bridge, I told myself to simply enjoy it.

As usual, Bob was soon attracting a lot of attention. There was a real party atmosphere and a lot of the charity fundraisers began taking snaps of him as we walked. He wasn't in the friendliest of moods, which was understandable. It was way past his bed time and he could feel the cold coming off the Thames. But I had a generous supply of snacks as well as some water and a bowl for him. I'd also been assured there would be a bowl of milk at the stop-off points. We will give it our best shot, I said to myself.

Bob and I settled into a group in the middle of the procession as it worked its way along the riverside. They were a mix of students and charity workers, as well as a couple of middle-aged women. They were obviously genuine people who wanted to help in some way. One of the ladies started asking me questions, the usual things: 'where do you come from?', 'how did you end up on the streets?'

I'd told the story a hundred times before during the past decade. I explained how I'd come to London from Australia when I was 18. I'd been born in the UK but my parents had separated and my mum had taken me with her when she'd moved down under. We'd moved around a lot in the following years and I'd become a bit of a trouble-maker. When I came to London I had hopes of making it as a musician, but it didn't really work out. I'd been staying with my stepsister but had fallen out with her husband. I'd started sleeping on friends' sofas but had eventually run out of places to crash the night. I'd ended up on the streets and it had been downhill from there. I'd experimented with drugs before but when I became homeless it became a way of life. It was the only way to block out the fact that I was lonely and that my life was screwed up. It anaesthetised the pain.

While we were talking we passed a building near Waterloo Bridge where I remembered sleeping a few times. 'I didn't use it often,' I told the lady, pointing it out. 'One night while I was crashing out there another guy got robbed and had his throat slashed while he slept.'

She looked at me ashen-faced.

'Did he die?' she said.

'I don't know. I just ran away,' I said. 'To be honest, you just worry about making it through the night yourself. It's every man for himself. That's what life on the streets reduces you to.'

The woman stood there just looking at the doorway for a moment, as if she was saying a brief, silent prayer.

After about an hour and a half, we made it to the first stopping off point – the Hispaniola floating restaurant on the Embankment on the north side of the Thames.

I helped myself to some of the soup on offer while Bob lapped up some milk that someone had kindly sorted out for him. I was feeling pretty positive about the whole thing and was already totting up the miles that I'd done – and how many more were to come.

But then, as we were heading off the ship, we had a bit of a setback. Perhaps because he'd been refuelled or perhaps because he knew that my leg still wasn't 100 per cent, Bob had decided to walk off the boat. As he padded his way down the ramp, right to the end of his lead, he walked straight into another *The Big Issue* seller who was coming up the walkway with a dog, a Staffie. It instantly went for Bob and I had to jump in front of it with my arms and legs out to stop him lunging at Bob. To be fair to the other guy, he gave his dog a real dressing down and even gave him a slap on the nose. Staffies do get a bad reputation for being violent, but I don't think this one was. He was just being curious, not evil. Unfortunately, however, it freaked Bob out a bit. As we resumed our walk he wrapped himself around me tightly, partly through nervousness but mostly because it was his way of insulating himself against the cold. There was a bone-chilling mist rising off the Thames.

Part of me wanted to call it a night and take Bob home. But I spoke to a couple of the organisers and was persuaded to carry on. Fortunately, as we headed away from the river, the temperatures lifted a little bit. We wound our way through the West End and headed north.

I got talking to another couple, a pretty young blonde girl and her French boyfriend. They were more interested in the story of how Bob and I had got together. That suited me fine. Walking around London like this brought back so many memories, many of them too dark and distressing for words. As a heroin addict living on the streets, I was reduced to doing some hideous things just to survive. I wasn't in the mood to share those details with anyone.

For the first six miles or so, my leg had been fine. I'd been too distracted by what was going on around me to think about it. But as the night wore on, I began to feel a throbbing pain in my thigh, where the DVT had been. It was inevitable. But it was still annoying.

For the next hour or so I ignored it. But whenever we stopped for a cup of tea I could feel an acute shooting pain. Early on I had been in the middle of the procession, walking along with the largest numbers of fundraisers. But I had been falling further and further behind, eventually reaching the back of the line. A couple of fundraisers and a guy from *The Big Issue* office were bringing up the rear and I tagged along with them for a mile or so. But I'd had to take a couple of breaks to let Bob do his business and have a cigarette. Suddenly I realised that we were now cut loose from the rest.

The next official stop was up in Camden, at the Roundhouse pub, a few miles away. I really didn't think I could make it that far. So when we passed a bus stop with a night bus that headed in our direction, I made a decision.

'What do you think, Bob, shall we call it quits?'

He didn't say anything, but I could tell that he was ready for his bed. When a bus loomed into view and opened its doors, he bounded on board and on to a seat, bristling with pleasure at being in the warm.

The bus was surprisingly busy given it was well after 3am. Sitting towards the back of the bus, Bob and I were surrounded by a cluster of clubbers, still high from their night out in the West End or wherever it was they'd been. There were also a couple of lonely looking guys sitting there as if they were on the road to nowhere. I'd been there and done that, of course. I not only had the t-shirt, I had a wardrobe full of them.

But that was the past. Tonight it felt very different. Tonight I felt rather pleased with myself. I know walking a dozen or so miles might not have seemed much of an achievement to some people, but to have made it that far given the state my leg had been in weeks earlier, was – for me, at least – the equivalent of running the London Marathon.

I'd also been reunited with some familiar faces, in particular, Billie. It had been a joy to see her again and to see how well she was doing. All in all, I just felt like I'd done something positive, that I'd given something back. I'd spent so many years taking from people, mainly because I had nothing to give. Or at least, I didn't think I had anything to give. Tonight had shown me that wasn't necessarily true. Everyone has something to contribute, no matter how small. Sharing my experiences tonight, for instance, I'd felt like I'd connected with a few people and, maybe, I'd opened their eyes to the reality of life on the streets. That wasn't to be dismissed. It was worth something. And so, I began to quietly tell myself, was I.

Chapter 10

Tales of Two Cities

As I drew back the bedroom curtains and looked out across the north London rooftops, it was obvious the Wintry weather the forecasters had been predicting had finished its journey from Siberia or whichever frozen wasteland had sent it in our direction.

Thick banks of iron-grey clouds were stacked up overhead and I could hear the wind gusting and whistling outside. If ever there was a day to stay at home and wrap up warm, today was that day. Unfortunately, that wasn't a luxury I could really afford.

Things were particularly tight at the moment. Both the gas and electric meters needed topping up so the flat was icy cold. Bob had got into the habit of snuggling up close to the bed at night, hoping to soak up some of the heat that I generated under the duvet. For now, at least, the bottom line was that I had to keep selling *The Big Issue* and I couldn't afford to take many days off – even if the weather looked as unpleasant as it did today.

So as I got my rucksack sorted the only question was whether Bob was going to come with me. As always, it was going to be his decision. I knew it was a decision he generally got right.

Cats – like a lot of other animals – are very good at 'reading' the weather and other natural events. Apparently they are very skilled at predicting earthquakes and tsunamis, for instance. The most likely explanation I've heard is that they are sensitive to air pressure. So it follows that they can also detect the changes in the air that predict bad weather is coming. Bob had certainly shown an aptitude for detecting that rain was in the air. He hated getting wet and had often curled up and refused to come out when the weather had been seemingly fine outside only for the heavens to open an hour or two later when I'd taken to the streets on my own.

So when I showed him his lead and scarf and he came towards me as normal, I guessed that his weather forecasting instincts were telling him it was safe to venture out.

'You sure about this, Bob?' I said. 'I'm happy to go on my own today.'

I picked out one of his thickest and warmest scarves. I wrapped it snugly around his neck and headed out into the greyness.

The moment I set foot on the street outside the wind cut through me like a scalpel. It pinched. I felt Bob's midriff curling itself even tighter than usual around my neck.

I dreaded having to wait at the bus stop for half an hour, but fortunately our regular service appeared within a few minutes and Bob and I were soon on board. Feeling a warmth on the back of my leg from a heater lifted my spirits briefly. But things soon took a turn for the worse.

We'd barely been on the road for ten minutes when I noticed the first flakes of snow swirling around outside. At first they were few and far between, but within what seemed like a few moments, the air was thick with chunky, white flakes that I could see were already sticking to the pavement and the roofs of parked cars.

'This doesn't look good,' I said to Bob, who was transfixed by the transformation that was taking place on the streets outside.

By the time we got to Newington Green, a mile or so from Angel, the traffic had ground to an almost total standstill. I faced a real Catch 22 – I knew it was going to be tough to earn a few quid today and that conditions were going to be really challenging but at the same time, I was so short of money. I wasn't sure I had enough to get back home, let alone put a few quid in the electricity meter over the next day or so.

'Come on, Bob, if we're going to earn anything today we'd better walk the last mile,' I said, reluctantly.

We hopped out on to the pavement to discover everyone was walking at a snail's pace, looking grim-faced as they picked their way along what was becoming a really treacherous surface. For Bob, however, this was a fascinating new world, one that he was soon eager to explore. I had put him on my shoulders as usual, but I'd barely walked a few yards before he was repositioning himself ready to clamber down to earth.

It hadn't really occurred to me, but as I put him down I realised that it was the first time Bob had been out and about in snow, with me, at least. I stood there watching him dabbing a paw into the powdery whiteness then standing back to admire the print he'd left in the virgin surface. For a moment I imagined what it must be like to see the world through his eyes. It must have seemed so bizarre to see everything suddenly turned white.

'Come on, mate, we can't hang around all day,' I said after a minute or two.

By now the snow was so heavy, it was hard to see in front of us.

Bob was still having a great time lifting his feet up in and out of the ever deepening snow. Eventually, however, it got so deep that his belly was lined with white crystals.

'Come on, mate, let's get you back up here,' I said, grabbing him and sticking back on my shoulders.

The problem now was that the snow was falling so steadily and heavily that it was settling on both of us. Every few yards I had to brush an inch of fresh snow off my shoulders then do the same thing to Bob.

I had a rather knackered old umbrella which I produced from my rucksack. But it was next to useless in the strong winds so I gave up on it within minutes.

'This is no good, Bob. Think we need to find you a coat,' I said. I dived into a small convenience store, stamping my feet clean of snow in the doorway.

At first the owner, an Indian lady, looked shocked to see the pair of us standing there, which was hardly surprising really. We must have made a bizarre sight. But her mood soon thawed.

'You are brave walking about in this weather,' she smiled.

'I don't know about brave,' I said. 'Mad might be closer to the truth.'

I wasn't quite sure what I was looking for. At first I wondered about buying a new umbrella, but they were too expensive for me. I only had a small amount of change. But then I had an idea and headed for the area where the kitchen supplies were stocked. I saw a roll of small, heavy duty bin liners.

'That might do the trick, Bob,' I said quietly.

'How much for a single bag?' I asked.

'I can't sell them as singles. I have to sell you the whole roll. It's £2,' she said.

I didn't want to fork out that much. I really was broke. But then I noticed she had little black carrier bags on the counter top for customers to carry their shopping.

'Is there any chance I could take one of those?' I said.

'OK,' she said, looking sheepishly at me. 'They are 5p.'

'OK, I'll take one. Do you have any scissors?'

'Scissors?'

'Yes, I want to make a hole in it.'

This time she looked at me as if I truly was off my rocker. But, probably against her better instinct, she dipped down behind the counter and produced a small pair of sewing scissors.

'Perfect,' I said.

I grabbed the closed end of the bag and cut a small semi-circle about the size of Bob's head. I then opened the bag up and slipped Bob's head through it. The improvised poncho fitted like a glove and covered his body and legs perfectly.

'Oh, I see,' the lady said, laughing. 'Very clever. That should do the trick.'

It took us about fifteen minutes to get to Angel. One or two people shot us funny looks as we walked along, but to be honest most were more concerned with getting from A to B safely in the drifting snow.

I knew there was no way we were going to be able to survive outside the tube at our normal pitch. The pavement was thick with slushy snow. So Bob and I positioned ourselves in the nearest underpass where the bulk of commuters were taking refuge.

I really didn't want to keep Bob out in the cold for too long, so I put some extra effort into selling the magazine. Fortunately, a lot of people seemed to take pity on us and dipped into their pockets. My pile of magazines was soon dwindling.

By late afternoon, I'd accumulated enough cash to keep us going for a day or two, I reckoned. The main thing was that I had enough to keep the gas and electricity topped up until, hopefully, the weather improved.

'Now, all we've got to do is get home,' I said to Bob as we once more bent ourselves into the icy winds and headed back to the bus stop.

There have to be easier ways of earning a crust than this, I told myself in the warmth of the bus.

Making money was so hard, especially because the gap between those that had it and those that didn't was growing ever greater. Working on the streets of London really was a tale of two cities, as I was reminded again a few days later.

I was standing just outside the concourse of Angel tube station with Bob on my shoulders around lunchtime, when I noticed a bit of a commotion going on inside at the ticket gate where passengers emerged from the trains below. A group of people were having an animated conversation with the attendants. When it was over they were let through seemingly without paying and started heading in our direction.

I recognised the large, slightly scruffy, blond-haired figure at the centre of the group immediately. It was the Mayor of London, Boris Johnson. He was with a young boy, his son I assumed, and a small group of smartly-dressed assistants. They were marching straight towards my exit.

I didn't really have time to think so I just reacted instinctively as he approached me.

'How about a *Big Issue*, Boris?' I said, waving a magazine in the air.

'I'm in a bit of a rush,' he said, looking flustered. 'Hold on.'

To his credit he started digging around in his pockets and produced a pile of coins which he then proceeded to drop into my hands.

'There you go. More valuable than British pounds,' he said.

I didn't understand what he meant but was grateful nevertheless.

'Thanks very much indeed for supporting Bob and me,' I said, handing him a magazine.

As he took it, he smiled and tilted his head slightly at Bob.

'That's a nice cat you've got there,' he said.

'Oh yes, he's a star, he's even got his own travel-card so he can travel around,' I said.

'Amazing. Really,' he said, before heading off in the direction of Islington Green with his entourage.

'Good luck, Boris,' I said as he disappeared from view.

I hadn't wanted to be rude and check what he'd given me a moment or two earlier, but, judging by the weight and number of the coins, it felt way more than the cover price of the magazine.

'That was generous of him wasn't it, Bob?' I said, fishing around for the coins which I'd hurriedly stuffed in my jacket pocket.

As I looked at the small pile of cash, however, my heart sank. The coins all bore the mark *Confoederatio Helvetica*.

'Oh no, Bob,' I said. 'He gave me bloody Swiss Francs.'

It was only then that the penny dropped, as it were.

'That's what he meant when he said *more valuable than British pounds*,' I muttered to myself.

Except, of course, they weren't more valuable.

It obviously hadn't occurred to him that, while foreign bank notes can be exchanged at most banks and bureaux de change, coins cannot. They were, effectively, worthless. To me, at least.

One of our friends at the tube station, Davika, passed by a moment or two later.

'Saw you with Boris, James,' she smiled. 'Did he see you all right?'

'No he didn't as a matter of fact,' I said. ' He gave me a pile of Swiss Francs.'

She shook her head.

'That's the rich for you,' she said. 'They live on a different planet from the rest of us.'

I just nodded quietly in agreement. It wasn't the first time something like this had happened to me.

A few years earlier, I'd been busking in Covent Garden. It had been approaching 7.30pm, curtain-up time at most of the theatres and opera houses in the area, and a lot of people were breaking into a panicky trot as they emerged from the tube station. Unsurprisingly, few of them had any time to notice me strumming away with Bob at my feet, but one particularly flustered looking character in a bow tie did acknowledge me.

He saw me from a few yards away and instantly dug into his pocket. He was a very grand looking character with a mane of grey hair. I could have sworn I recognised him from the television, but couldn't place him. When I saw him reach into his trouser pocket and pull out a scrunched up note, I thought my luck was in. It was red and looked all the world like a big denomination, possibly a £50 note. That was the only note I knew that had red in it.

'There you go, my man,' he said, thrusting it into my hand as he slowed down for a brief moment.

'Cheers. Thanks very much indeed,' I said.

'Have a good evening,' he said, laughing as he picked up speed again and ran towards the Piazza.

I had no idea why he was laughing. I assumed he was in a good mood.

I waited a few minutes until the crowds had died down a little before recovering the scrunched up note out of my pocket.

It didn't take me long to work out that it wasn't a £50 note. As I'd thought, it was red, but it had a picture of a bearded bloke I'd never seen before on it. It had the number 100 written on it. The writing was in some kind of Eastern European language. The only word that looked familiar was *Srbije*. I had no idea what it was or what it might be worth. It might have been more than £50 for all I knew. So I packed up my stuff and headed for a Bureau de Change the other side of the Piazza which I knew was open late for tourists.

'Hi, can you tell me what this is worth, please?' I said to the girl who was behind the window.

She looked at it and gave me a puzzled look.

'Don't recognise it, hold on, let me check with someone else,' she said.

She went into a back office where I could see an older bloke sitting.

After a short confab she came back.

'Apparently it's Serbian, it's 100 Serbian dinar,' she said.

'OK,' I said. 'Can I exchange it?'

'Let's see what it's worth,' she said tapping away at a computer and then a calculator.

'Hmmm,' she said. 'That comes out at just over 70p. So we wouldn't be able to exchange it.'

I felt disappointed. I'd secretly hoped that it might be enough money to get me and Bob through the weekend. Fat chance. There were times when I got really depressed by the predicament I found myself in. I had turned 30. The majority of guys of my age had a job or a car, a home and a pension plan, maybe even a wife and a few children. I had none of those things. Part of me didn't actually want them, truth be told. But I did yearn for the security that some of those things brought. I was fed up with living off my wits on the streets. And I was fed up with being humiliated by those who had absolutely no concept of – nor sometimes any sympathy for – the life I was having to lead. There were times when I felt like I was close to breaking point. A few days after that incident with the Mayor, I felt like I had reached it.

Bob and I finished work early and headed down to the tube, jumping on a Northern line train to Euston then switching on to the Victoria line to Victoria Station. As we weaved our way through the tunnels, Bob walked ahead of me on his lead part of the way. He knew where we were heading.

We were meeting my father, something I'd begun to do more regularly in recent months. Relations between us had been pretty fraught in the past. When my parents had separated, my mother had won custody and taken me to live on the other side of the world, in Australia, so he'd barely known me when I was growing up as a little boy. By the time I'd come to London as a teenager, I was a real handful. Within a year of getting here, I had disappeared off the face of the earth and started sleeping rough. When I'd resurfaced, he'd tried to help me get back on track, but, to be honest, I had been almost beyond salvation.

We'd become a bit closer when I'd started cleaning up my act a little and had got into the habit of meeting for a few drinks at a pub at Victoria Station. The staff there were pretty friendly and would let me slip Bob in provided I kept him hidden from the other punters. I'd learned to keep him under a table where he was happy snoozing. It was a cheap and cheerful place and we'd usually have a meal as well. It was always my dad's treat. Well, I was never going to have the money to treat him, was I?

As usual, he was waiting there for me.

'So what's your news?'

'Not a lot,' I said. 'I'm getting cheesed off with selling *The Big Issue*. It's too dangerous. And London is full of people who don't give a sh*t about you.'

I then told him the story about Boris Johnson. He gave me a sympathetic look but his reply was predictable.

'You need to get yourself cleaned up and you need to get yourself a proper job, Jamie,' he said. (He was the only person who called me that.)

I resisted the temptation to roll my eyes.

'That's easier said than done, Dad,' I said.

My dad had always been a grafter, a hard worker. He was blue collar to the core. He'd graduated from being an antique dealer to having a washing machine and domestic appliance repair service to a mobility vehicle business. He'd always been his own boss. I don't think he quite grasped why I hadn't been able to do the same thing. To his credit, he had never washed his hands of me. He'd tried to help. At one point I had been keen on getting into music production and he'd wanted to give me a helping hand to get on a course but it hadn't panned out. The thought was there but the motion behind it wasn't. He had remarried since splitting with my mum and had two children, my half siblings Caroline and Anthony, to look after. It got complicated.

I'd never really considered working for his business and he'd never really offered. Quite rightly, he felt that business and family didn't mix. Besides, deep down he knew that I wasn't reliable – or presentable – enough to interact with the public.

'What about training in computing or something like that. There are loads of courses around,' he said.

This was true enough but I didn't have the qualifications to get on most courses. That was partly my own fault.

A few years back I'd had a mentor, a great guy called Nick Ransom who worked for a charity called Family Mosaic. He had been a really good friend. He'd either come to my flat or I'd go into his office in Dalston where he'd help me with everything from paying the bills to applying for jobs. He had tried to get me involved in a variety of courses, from bike building to computing. But the struggle to kick my addiction had been all consuming and I'd never knuckled down to it. Busking had always been an easier option for me and when

Nick moved on to pastures new the chance slipped through my fingers. It wasn't the first opportunity I'd messed up, nor would it be the last.

My dad said he'd ask around to see if there was anything going. 'But things are pretty rough everywhere at the moment,' he said, holding up a copy of the evening paper. 'Every time I look at the paper it's all doom and gloom. Jobs going everywhere.'

I wasn't that disconnected from reality. I knew there were millions of people in the same situation as me, every single one of them with better qualifications. I was so far down the pecking order in the jobs market I felt that it wasn't even worth applying for jobs.

My dad wasn't a man to bare his emotions with me. I knew he was frustrated by the way I lived my life. Deep down I knew he felt I wasn't trying. I understood why he felt that way, but the truth was that I was trying. Just in my own way.

To lighten things up a little we talked a little bit about his family. I wasn't particularly close to Anthony and Caroline; we met very infrequently. He asked me what I was doing for Christmas – I'd spent a couple of Christmases with him but it hadn't really been a barrel of laughs for either of us.

'I'm just going to spend it with Bob,' I said. 'We enjoy being together.'

My dad didn't really get my relationship with Bob. Tonight, as usual, he stroked him occasionally and kept an eye on him when I popped to the toilet. He even got the waitress to bring him a saucer of milk and gave him a couple of snacks. But he wasn't a natural cat lover. And on the one or two occasions when I had talked about how much Bob helped me in sorting myself out he just looked baffled. I suppose I couldn't blame him for that.

As usual, my Dad asked after 'my health' which I always took to be code for 'are you still off the drugs?'

'I'm doing all right,' I said. 'I saw a guy drop dead from an overdose on the landing of my flats a while back. That freaked me out quite a lot.'

He looked horrified. He had no understanding of drug culture or the way it worked and, like a lot of men of his generation, was a little bit scared of it truth be told. For that reason, I don't think he'd ever really grasped how bad my situation had been when I'd been at my lowest ebb on heroin.

He'd seen me during that period, but, like all addicts, I had learned to keep that side of my life hidden when necessary. I'd met him a couple of times when I was off my face on gear. I'd just told him I had a bout of the flu and assumed he wouldn't know any different. He wasn't stupid though, he probably sensed something was wrong but wouldn't have been able to put his finger on what it was specifically. He had no concept of what it was like to do drugs. I quite envied him that.

We spent an hour and a half together, but then he had to catch a train back to south London. He gave me a few quid to tide me over and we agreed to see each other again in a few weeks' time.

'Look after yourself, Jamie,' he said.

The station was still busy. It was the back end of the rush hour. I had a few magazines left in my satchel so decided to try and shift them before heading home. I found an empty pitch outside the railway station and was soon doing pretty well.

Bob had a full stomach and was on good form. People were stopping and making a fuss. I was just weighing up whether to spend the money I was making on a takeaway curry when trouble reared its head again.

I knew the pair were trouble the moment I set eyes on them heading across the road towards the main entrance to Victoria Station. I recognised one of them from my days selling *The Big Issue* in Covent Garden. He was a wiry, grey-haired guy in his mid-forties. He was wearing the distinctive, red tabard but I knew he wasn't a legitimate seller. He had been 'de-badged' a long time ago for various misdemeanours. His mate wasn't familiar, but I didn't need to know him to be able to tell he was a rough character. He was a big brute and was built like a sack of potatoes.

I immediately worked out what they were doing.

The smaller one was waving a single copy of *The Big Issue* around, stopping people, collecting money but never handing over the magazine. They were running a scam called One Booking, in which vendors used a single, out-of-date magazine to generate a string of sales. Each time someone handed over some money, the seller would come out with some sob story about it being their last copy and being in particularly dire straits. It was begging, basically. There was no other word for it.

I was always amazed that anyone fell for it. But there were always a few gullible – or maybe generous – souls around.

I was worried that they were heading in our direction. Sure enough, they were soon outside the tube station entrance, with the smaller of the pair approaching travellers on the edge of the steps. It was blindingly obvious he wasn't an official seller. The tabard was ripped to shreds and looked like it had been pulled out of a dustbin. It was also missing the official badge that legitimate vendors wore on the left hand side of their vests.

As his mate went about his business, the bigger of the two made a bee-line for me. He was every bit as aggressive as he looked.

'Oi, you, get lost, or I'll kill that cat of yours,' he said, sticking his big red face close to mine. There was a trace of Irish in his accent and his breath stank of booze.

Bob, as always, had spotted the danger and was hissing at him already. I knelt down and got him to climb on my shoulders before there was any trouble.

I wasn't going to be intimidated and stuck my ground.

'I've got a right to sell here and I've just got these few magazines to sell,' I said. 'You know what you are doing is wrong. You are nothing but a leech, you are forcing him to beg for you.'

He didn't like this and warned me again.

'You've got two minutes to pack your stuff up and f*** off,' he said, temporarily distracted by his mate who was waving to him for some reason. He then pushed his way into the crowds.

People were flooding in and out of the station, so I lost them for a few minutes. I knew the score. They were both drug addicts and were only running this scam until they had enough money to head off and fix themselves up. I was hoping that his mate's signal indicated that they'd hit their target and were going to disappear. No such luck.

In hardly any time, the big guy reappeared, looking even angrier than before. He was literally frothing at the mouth and spitting out expletives. 'Didn't you hear what I told you?' he snarled.

The next thing I knew he had hit me. He just walked up to me and punched me on the nose. It happened so fast, I didn't even see him pull back his arm. He just jabbed a giant fist into my face. I didn't have a hope of deflecting the blow.

'What the hell?' I said, back-pedalling, Bob hanging on for dear life.

When I drew my hand away from my face I could see that it was covered in blood. It was gushing out and my nose felt like it had some broken cartilage in there.

I decided it wasn't a fight I could win. There was no sign of the Police so I was on my own against a pretty nasty pair of individuals.

Working on the streets was risky, I knew that. But there were times when it was downright dangerous. I'd heard stories of *Big Issue* sellers being killed. There had been a case up in Norwich where two or three guys set about a vendor there and kicked him to death. I really didn't want to add to the statistics.

'Come on, Bob, let's get out of here,' I said, grabbing my stuff and heading off.

I felt a mix of anger and despair. I was desperate for a change in my fortunes. I didn't think I could take much more of this life. But, try as I might, I couldn't see how on earth I was going to break free. Suddenly all that talk with my father of jobs and training seemed ridiculous, a complete pipe dream. Who was going to pay a recovering junkie a decent salary? Who was going to hire someone with a curriculum vitae as barren as the Australian outback where I spent part of my childhood? On that day, feeling as low as I did, the answer was as plain and bloody obvious as the nose on my face: no one.

Chapter 11

Two Cool Cats

One lunchtime in September 2010, I arrived at Angel tube to be greeted by Davika. She was a ticket attendant and had been one of our most loyal friends since Bob and I had started working in Islington. She often brought Bob a little treat or something to drink, especially during hot weather. Today, however, she simply wanted to deliver a message.

'Hi James, there was someone here looking for you and Bob,' she said. 'He was a reporter from one of the local papers. He asked me to call him back if you were willing to talk to him.'

'Really?' I said. 'I guess I don't mind. Tell him he can come and see us during our regular hours.'

It wasn't the first time someone had paid us attention. There were a couple of films on the internet about Bob and I that had been viewed by a few thousand people and a couple of London bloggers had written nice things about us, but no one from the newspapers had shown any interest. To be honest, I took it with a pinch of salt. I'd had all sorts of weird and wonderful approaches over the years, 99 per cent of which came to nought.

A couple of days later, however, I arrived at Angel to find this guy outside the tube station waiting for us.

'Hi James, my name is Peter,' he said. 'I was wondering if I could do an interview with you for the *Islington Tribune*?'

'Sure, why not?'

He proceeded to take a picture of Bob perched on my shoulder with the Angel tube station sign behind us. I felt a bit self-conscious. I hadn't exactly dressed up for the occasion and was wearing a thick, early winter's beard, but he seemed happy enough with the results.

We then had a bit of a chat about my past and how we'd met. It wasn't quite the Spanish inquisition, but it clearly gave him enough ammunition for his piece which he said would appear in the next edition of the *Tribune*. Again, I didn't really take it too seriously. I worked on the principle that I'd believe it when I saw it. It was easier that way.

It was a few days later on a Thursday morning, that Rita and Lee, the co-ordinators at *The Big Issue* stall on Islington Green called me over.

'Hey James, you and Bob are in the paper today,' Rita said, producing a copy of the *Tribune*.

'Are we?' I asked.

Sure enough there was a half-page article on us written by Peter Gruner. The headline read:

TWO COOL CATS . . .
THE BIG ISSUE SELLER
AND A STRAY CALLED BOB.

The story began:

> Not since the legendary Dick Whittington has a man and his cat become such unlikely celebrities on the streets of Islington. *The Big Issue* seller James Bowen and his docile ginger cat Bob, who go everywhere together, have been attracting comments since they first appeared outside Angel Tube station. The story of how they met – widely reported in blogs on the internet – is one of such extraordinary pathos that it seems only a matter of time before we get a Hollywood film.

I had to laugh out loud at some of the journalistic licence. Dick Whittington? Hollywood film? And I wasn't terribly pleased with the way I looked in the photo, sporting that thick beard. But it was a lovely piece, I had to admit.

I popped into the newsagent and grabbed a few copies to take home. Bob saw me looking at the piece again on the bus that evening and did a kind of double take. It didn't happen very often, but for a split second he had this slightly baffled expression on his face. It was as if he was saying: 'No, it can't be. Can it? Really?'

Plenty of people knew it was really us though. And the publicity was soon reaping dividends, if only small ones. I'd agreed to do the interview mainly because I thought it would be good for sales of my magazines. I thought that by raising my profile it might encourage a few more customers to stop and talk to me at Angel tube station. And it did. In the days that followed, more and more people started saying hello to us not only at Angel, but on the bus and on the street.

One morning I was taking Bob to do his business on Islington Green when a group of school-children appeared in front of us. They could only have been about nine or ten-years-old and were in very smart, blue uniforms.

'Look, it's Bob,' one of them, a little boy, said, pointing excitedly.

It was clear the rest of the class didn't have a clue what he was talking about.

'Who's Bob?' a voice asked.

'That cat there on that man's shoulders. He's famous. My mum says he looks like Garfield,' the boy said.

I was touched that we were being recognised

by young children but I wasn't quite so sure I was happy about the comparison with the world's best-known cartoon cat. Garfield was famous for being obese, obsessed with eating, lazy and slightly obnoxious. He also hated any form of exercise or hard work. Bob had always been in fine fettle, ate pretty sensibly and had the friendliest, most laid back attitude of any cat I'd ever come across. And no one could ever call him work-shy.

There were lots of similar encounters during the days after the piece was published, but the most significant came from someone I'd spoken to once before.

I'd already been approached one evening by an American lady who said she was a literary agent. Her name was Mary. She told me she lived nearby and had noticed Bob and I outside the tube station many times.

She'd asked me if I had considered writing a book about my life with Bob. I said I would think about it, but, truth be told, I hadn't really taken her seriously. How could I? I was a recovering drug addict who was struggling to survive selling *The Big Issue*. I didn't write a diary. I didn't even write texts on my mobile phone. Yes, I loved to read and consumed all the books I could lay my hands on. But, as far as I could see, at least, writing a book was about as realistic as building myself a space rocket or running for Parliament. In other words, it was a complete and utter non-starter.

Fortunately, she'd persisted and we'd spoken again. She had anticipated my concerns and suggested that I meet a writer who was experienced at helping people tell their stories. She told me he was busy at the time, but that he would be free towards the end of the year and would come and see me. After the *Islington Tribune* piece she contacted me again to confirm that I was happy to meet him.

If he thought there was a book in Bob and me, he would spend time with me, getting me to tell my story then helping to shape it up and write it. She would then try and sell it to a publisher. Again, it sounded too far-fetched for words.

I didn't hear anything for a while, but then, towards the end of November, I got a call from this writer guy. His name was Garry.

I agreed to meet him and he took me for a coffee in the Design Centre across the road from my pitch. We had Bob with us, so we had to sit outdoors in the biting cold. Bob was a better judge of character than me, so I made a point of going to the toilet and leaving them alone a couple of times. They got on famously, which I took to be a good omen.

I could tell he was trying to work out whether my story was suitable for a book and was as open as I felt was possible.

As far as I was concerned, I really didn't want to have to go into the dark side of my life. But as we spoke, he said something that struck a chord. He could see that Bob and I were both broken souls. We'd come together when we were both at rock bottom. We'd helped mend each other's lives.

'That's the story you have to tell,' he told me.

I had never thought of it in those terms. Instinctively, I knew that Bob had been a hugely positive force in my life. I'd even seen me on a video on YouTube saying that he'd saved my life. I guessed that, to some extent, it was true. But I just couldn't imagine that being a story that would interest anyone.

Even when I had seen Garry again for another, longer chat, it all seemed a bit of a pipe dream. There were so many ifs and maybes. If Garry and Mary were willing to work with me, maybe a publisher would be interested in releasing a book. I really couldn't see all three of those things happening. The obstacles seemed too great. As the festive season and the end of the year loomed into view, I told myself there was more chance of Father Christmas being real. Bob and I had grown to love Christmas together. The first year we'd been together we'd spent it alone in the flat, sharing a couple of ready meals and watching TV. Given that I'd spent several of the past ten Christmases on my own, in a hostel or off my face on heroin, it had felt like the happiest holiday ever.

I'd missed the second one by travelling to Australia, but ever since then we'd been together.

During the run up to Christmas, we had, as usual, been given a host of presents, from scarves for Bob to gift certificates for both of us at shops like Sainsbury's, Marks and Spencer and H&M. There was no question about which was Bob's favourite: an advent calendar filled with his favourite treats. He'd fallen in love with it instantly, naturally, and had quickly learned to make a fuss first thing in the morning when it was time to produce the latest snack on the countdown to Christmas.

We also got a fantastic Santa Paws outfit. Belle had made me one for our very first Christmas together but it had somehow got lost. This one had a snug red jacket and a very striking red hat for Bob to wear during the festive season. Passers-by at Angel were besotted by it.

When it came to Christmas Day itself Bob spent more time playing with the wrapping paper than the actual present itself. He rolled around on the carpet, nibbling at it. I left him to it and spent the afternoon watching television and playing video games. Belle popped round for a few hours. It felt like a real family Christmas to me.

It was a couple of weeks into the New Year when I got a phone call from Mary telling me that a major London publisher, Hodder and Stoughton, wanted to meet me – and Bob, of course.

A few days later, I went along to their offices in a rather grand tower block near Tottenham Court Road. At first, the security people weren't going to let Bob into the building. They looked baffled when we said he was going to be the subject of a book. I could see their point. Hodder's other authors included people like John Grisham and Gordon Ramsay. What on earth would they be doing publishing a book about a scruffy-looking bloke and his ginger tom cat?

Someone from the publishers came down to sort it out, however, and after that Bob and I were both made to feel very welcome. In fact Bob was treated like visiting royalty. He was given a little goodie bag with some little snacks and catnip toys and allowed to wander around the offices exploring. Wherever he went he was greeted like some kind of celebrity. People were snapping away on their phones and cooing over him. I knew he had star quality but I didn't realise it was this potent.

I, on the other hand, had to sit in on a meeting in which a long line of people popped in to talk about their different specialities, from marketing and publicity to production and sales. There was all sorts of business talk about publishing dates and production schedules. They might as well have been talking Serbo-Croat or Mandarin. But the long and the short of it was that they had seen some of the material Garry and I had worked on and they wanted to publish a book based on it. Between them, they'd even come up with a title: *A Street Cat Named Bob*. Tennessee Williams may have been spinning in his grave, but I thought it was very clever.

Soon I was being asked to visit the literary agency where Mary worked over in Chelsea. Again, it was a very grand and slightly intimidating place. They were more used to welcoming Nobel and Booker prize winners so there were a few odd looks when people realised that a *Big Issue* seller and his cat had walked into their rarefied atmosphere. While Bob explored the offices, Mary ran me through the contract that I'd been offered by the publishers. She told me it was a good deal, especially given I was an 'unknown author'. I placed my trust in her and signed all the paperwork.

Over the course of the last ten years I'd been more used to signing drug prescriptions and police release forms. It felt weird scrawling my name, but also, I had to confess, very, very exciting.

There were times when I woke up in the morning thinking it was all a figment of my imagination. This couldn't really be happening. Not to me.

I didn't want Garry coming round to my flat at that point. So I began meeting him once or twice a week in Islington. There were pros and cons to the arrangement. On the plus side, it meant that I could top up my money and spend a few hours working afterwards. But it also meant that I had Bob with me, which meant that finding somewhere to sit and talk was a challenge, especially when the weather was bad. The local cafés wouldn't let a cat on the premises and there wasn't a library nearby. So we had to find alternatives.

The first people to invite us in from the cold, ironically, were Waterstones, the bookshop on Islington Green. They knew me in there. I'd often pop in with Bob to look through the Science Fiction section. The manager there, Alan, was on duty and we asked him if he minded us working upstairs in a quiet corner. He not only said yes, he got a member of staff to organise two chairs for us in the history section. He even brought a couple of coffees in.

When the sun was out, we used a place on the Essex Road that had tables outside. I could smoke there as well, which was a bonus for me.

Garry and I were determined that the book wouldn't just be about my life with Bob. We wanted it to offer people some insights into life on the streets. I wanted to get across to people how easy it was for people like me to fall through the cracks, to become forgotten and overlooked by society. Of course, in order to do that, I had to tell my 'back-story' as well.

I really wasn't looking forward to that part of the exercise. Talking about myself wasn't something that came easily to me, especially when it came to the darker stuff. And there was a lot of that. There were aspects of my life as an addict that I had buried away in the farthest corners of my mind. I'd made choices that I was deeply ashamed about, done things that I didn't want to share with anyone, let alone put in a book. But once we began talking, to my surprise, it was less painful than I'd feared. I couldn't afford to see a psychologist or a psycho-analyst but there were times when talking to Garry was as good as talking to a shrink. It forced me to confront some painful truths and was strangely cathartic, helping me to understand myself a little better.

I knew I wasn't the easiest person to deal with. I had a defiant, self-destructive streak that had

consistently got me into trouble. It was pretty obvious that I'd had a childhood that had messed me
up. My parents' divorce and my peripatetic years,
flitting between the UK and Australia, hadn't
exactly been stabilising forces. I'd always tried
really hard to fit in and be popular as a kid, but it
had never worked. I'd ended up trying too hard –
and become a misfit and an outcast as a result.

By the time I was an adolescent my behavioural
problems had begun. I was angry and rebellious
and fell out with my mother and stepfather. For a
period of around two years, between the ages of 11
and 13, I'd been constantly in and out of the
Princess Margaret Hospital for Children outside
Perth. At one point I'd been diagnosed as either
bi-polar or manic depressive. I can't remember
exactly which it was. They seemed to come up with
a new diagnosis every week. Either way, the upshot
was that I was prescribed various medications,
including lithium.

The memories from that time were mixed.

One vivid memory that sprung to mind was of
going into the surgery at the Princess Margaret for
a weekly blood test. The walls of the surgery were
plastered in posters of pop and rock stars so I had
the blood tests done while staring at a picture of
Gladys Knight and the Pips.

Each time the doctor assured me that the injec-
tion he was about to give me wouldn't hurt. 'It will

only feel like a scratch,' he'd say, but it was always more than that. It was kind of ironic, I suppose, but I'd had a phobia about needles for years after that. It was a measure of how deep my drug addiction had been that I'd somehow forgotten this and happily injected myself on a daily basis.

On a happier note, I remembered how, after leaving the hospital, I had wanted to give something back and had begun donating boxes of comic books. I'd managed to get myself some work experience in a comic book shop nearby and had persuaded the boss to let me take boxes of unsold magazines for the kids at the hospital. I'd spent many hours playing air hockey and watching video games in the activity room they had in the children's ward so I knew they'd all appreciate something decent to read.

In the main, however, the memories of that time were pretty grim. They opened my eyes to aspects of my youth that I'd never really examined before.

At one point, for instance, we were working on the book on the day after I'd watched a film by the documentary-maker Louis Theroux about how parents in America were using more and more psychoactive medication to treat their kids for disorders like ADHD, Asperger's and bipolar disorders.

It occurred to me suddenly that this was exactly what had happened to me. And it struck me that being treated like this must have had a huge impact on me when I was young. It made me wonder what had come first. It was a chicken and egg question: had I been given the drugs because I was acting up? Or did I start acting up because of all the visits to doctors who convinced me that there must be something wrong with me? Perhaps most scary of all, what effect did all that medication have on me and my young personality? As a young kid I'd considered myself quite a happy-go-lucky character, but since that time I had been what I suppose you'd call 'troubled'. I'd struggled to fit into society and suffered from depression and mood swings. Was there a link? I had no idea.

What I did know, however, was that I couldn't blame the doctors, my mother or anyone else for the way my life had gone since then. Yes, they had played a role, but the buck stopped with me. No one told me to develop a drug problem. No one forced me to drift on to the streets of London. No one made me take up heroin. They were mistakes that I made of my own free will. I hadn't needed anyone's help to screw up my life. I'd done a perfectly good job of that on my own.

If nothing else, the book was an opportunity for me to make that crystal clear.

For a moment my dad was lost for words. The expression on his face was a mixture of disbelief, happiness, pride – and mild apprehension.

'That's a lot of money, Jamie,' he said after a couple of moments, putting to one side the manila coloured cheque I'd just handed him.

'You'd better be careful with that.'

The reality of what had happened hadn't really sunk in until now. Not just for my dad, but for me either. There had been meetings with publishers, contracts signed, even articles in the newspapers. But it hadn't been until I received this cheque for the advance that it finally struck home.

When it had first flopped through the letter box a couple of days earlier, I had opened the envelope and then simply sat there looking at it. The only cheques I'd seen in the past decade had been from the DHSS. They were for small amounts, £50 here and £100 there, never anything with more than a couple of noughts on it.

Compared to some people, especially in London, it wasn't actually that large a sum of money. For a lot of the commuters walking past me each day on their way to the City of London, I guess it wasn't even a month's salary. But for someone for whom £60 was a very good day's wage, it was an eye-watering amount of cash.

The arrival of the cheque, though, had brought two immediate problems. I was terrified of frittering it away but, even more of a worry, I didn't have a bank account into which I could pay it. I'd had an account years ago but hadn't managed it very well. I'd got used to living on cash and for the last few years had taken all my cheques to a 'cash converters'. Which was why I'd travelled to my father's house in south London.

'I was hoping you could look after it for me,' I'd asked him over the phone. 'I can then ask you for money as and when I need it.'

He'd agreed and I'd now had the cheque endorsed over to his name. (Not a huge change because we shared the exact same initials and surname.)

Rather than meeting as usual at Victoria, he'd invited me over to his neck of the woods. We went for a couple of drinks in his local and chatted for a couple of hours.

'So is this going to be a proper book?' he asked me, the scepticism he'd displayed ever since I'd told him about it resurfacing once more.

'What do you mean?'

'Well, is it a picture book or a children's book? What is it going to be about exactly?' he said.

It was a fair question, I suppose.

I explained that it was the story of how I met Bob, and how we'd helped each other. He looked a little nonplussed.

'So will me and your mother be in it?' he asked.

'You might get a mention,' I said.

'I'd better get on to my lawyers then,' he said, smiling.

'No, don't worry. The only person that comes out badly in all this is me.'

That made him change tack a little.

'And is this going to be a long-term thing?' he continued. 'You writing books.'

'No,' I said, honestly. 'I'm not going to become the next J.K. Rowling dad. There are thousands of books published every year. Only a tiny minority of them become bestsellers. I really don't think a tale about a busker and recovering drug addict and his stray ginger cat is going to be one of them. So, yes this is going to be a short-term thing. It's a nice windfall, and no more.'

'All the more reason to be careful with the money then,' he said, seizing the opportunity to give me some sensible fatherly advice.

He was right, of course. This money would ease the stress on me for a few months, but not much longer. I had debts to clear and my flat was badly in need of some refurbishing. I knew I had to be realistic which meant that I had to keep my job with *The Big Issue* going. We talked about this for a little while, but he then went off into a lecture on the relative merits of various investments and savings schemes. At that point, I did what I had so often done when my parents spoke to me. I tuned out completely.

Chapter 12

The Joy of Bob

Being with Bob has been such an education. I'd not had many mentors in my life and had spurned the few well-meaning people who had tried to guide and advise me. I always knew better than them, or so I imagined.

It is a bizarre thing to admit, but with Bob it has been different. He has taught me as much, if not more, than any human I've come across. Since being in his company I've learned important lessons about everything from responsibility and friendship to selflessness. He has even given me an insight into a subject I thought I'd never really understand – parenthood.

I doubted whether I would ever have children. I wasn't sure whether I'd be up to the job and, truth be told, the opportunity hadn't really presented itself. I'd had a couple of girlfriends over the years, including Belle, to whom I was still really close and thought the world of. But starting a family hadn't ever been on the horizon. As Belle once succinctly put it, I was too busy behaving like a child myself most of the time.

Caring for Bob has, however, given me a glimpse into what it must be like to be a father. In particular, it has made me realise that parenthood is all about anxiety. Whether it is fretting over his health, watching out for him when we are out on the streets, or simply making sure he is warm and well fed, life with Bob often feels like one worry after another.

It actually chimes with something that my father had said to me after I'd been missing in London for a year or so. It had been at the height of my addiction and both he and my mother had been beside themselves with concern about me.

'You have no idea how much a parent worries about his or her child,' he had shouted at me, furious at what he called my selfishness in not being in touch with them.

It hadn't meant much at all to me then. Since being with Bob I have begun to appreciate what hell I must have put my parents through. I wish I could turn back the clock and save them all that grief.

That is the bad news. The good news is that, in amongst the anxiety and worry, 'parenthood' brings with it a lot of laughter too. That is another thing Bob has taught me. For far too long I'd found it hard to find much joy in life. He has taught me how to be happy again. Even the slightest, silliest moments we share together can bring an instant smile to my face.

One Saturday lunchtime, for instance, I answered a knock on the door and found the guy from the flat across the hallway standing there.

'Hi, just thought I'd let you know that your cat is out here.'

'Sorry, erm, no. Must be someone else's. Mine's in here,' I said, turning around to scout around the living room.

'Bob. Where are you?'

There was no sign of him.

'No, I'm pretty sure this is him out here. Ginger isn't he?' the guy said.

I stepped out into the hallway to discover Bob sitting around the corner, perfectly still on top of a cupboard on the landing with his head pressed against the window, looking down on the street below.

'He's been there a while. I noticed him earlier,' the guy said, heading for the lift.

'Oh. Thanks,' I said.

Bob just looked at me as if I was the world's biggest party pooper. The expression on his face seemed to say: 'Come on up here and take a look at this view with me, it's really interesting.'

'Bob, how the heck have you got there?' I said, reaching up to collect him.

Belle was visiting and was in the kitchen rustling up a sandwich.

'Did you let Bob out?' I asked her back inside the flat.

'No,' she said, looking up from the worktop.

'I can't work out how he got out into the hallway and hid himself up on top of the cupboard.'

'Ah, hold on,' Belle said, a light coming on somewhere inside her head. 'I popped downstairs about an hour ago to put some rubbish out. You were in the bathroom. I shut the door behind me but he must have slid out without me noticing and then hidden away somewhere when I came back up. He's so damned clever. I'd love to know what's going on in his mind sometimes.'

I couldn't help laughing out loud. It was a subject I'd speculated on quite a lot over the years. I'd often found myself imagining the thought processes Bob went through. I knew it was a pointless exercise and I was only projecting human behaviour onto an animal. Anthropomorphising I think they call it. But I couldn't resist it.

It wasn't hard, for instance, to work out why he'd been so happy finding his new vantage point out in the hallway today.

There was nothing Bob loved more than watching the world go by. Inside the flat, he would regularly position himself on the kitchen window sill. He could sit there happily all day, monitoring the goings on below, like some kind of security guard.

His head would follow people as they walked towards and then past our flats. If someone turned into the entrance to the building, he'd stretch himself until he had lost sight of them. It might sound crazy, but I found it incredibly entertaining. He took it so seriously that it was almost as if he had a list of people who were allowed to travel this way at certain times and in certain directions. He'd see someone passing and look as if to say 'yes, OK, I know who you are' or 'come on you're running late for the bus to work'. At other times he'd get quite agitated, as if he was thinking: 'Oi, hang on! I don't recognise you' or: 'Hey. You don't have clearance, where do you think you're going. Get back here.'

I could easily while away half an hour just watching Bob watching others. Belle and I used to joke that he was on patrol.

Bob's escape into the hallway today was typical of something else he seemed to love doing as well, playing hide and seek. I'd found him hiding in all sorts of surprising nooks and crannies. He particularly loved anywhere warm.

One evening, I went to have a bath before I went

to bed. As I nudged the bathroom door open, I couldn't help thinking it felt a little odd. Rather than swinging open easily it needed an extra nudge. It felt heavy somehow.

I didn't think much more of it and started running a bath. I was looking in the mirror by the sink when I noticed something moving on the back of the door amongst the towels I kept in a rack. It was Bob.

'How on earth have you got up there?' I said, howling with laughter.

I worked out that he must have climbed on to a shelving unit near the door and then, somehow, jumped from there on to the towels, pulling himself up on to the top of them. It looked pretty uncomfortable as well as precarious but he seemed really happy.

The bathroom was a favourite spot for hide and seek. Another frequent trick of his was to hide inside the clothes horse I often used to dry my washing in the bath tub, especially during winter.

Several times I'd been brushing my teeth or even sitting on the toilet, and suddenly noticed the clothes moving. Bob would then appear, pushing the clothes apart like curtains, his face wearing a sort of *peek-a-boo* expression. He thought it was great entertainment.

Bob's ability to get into trouble was another source of endless entertainment.

He loved watching television and computer screens. He could while away endless hours watching wildlife programmes or horse racing. He would sit there, as if he was mesmerised. So when we walked past the gleaming new Apple store in Covent Garden one afternoon, I thought I'd give him a treat. The place was bursting with shiny new laptops and desktops, none of which I could remotely afford. But the Apple philosophy was that anyone could stroll in and play around with their technology. So we did.

We had spent a few minutes playing with the computers, surfing the internet and watching YouTube videos when Bob spotted a screen that had a kind of aquarium-style display, with exotic and really colourful fish swimming around. I could see why he was attracted to it. It was absolutely stunning.

I took him over to the giant screen and let him gape at it for a few moments. It was funny to watch. He would follow a particular fish as it progressed around the screen and then disappeared. He would then do a sort of double take. He couldn't fathom what was happening and darted behind the giant screen, expecting to find the fish there. But when all he saw was a wall of silver and a tangle of leads, he darted back again and started following another fish.

It carried on like this for minutes until he suddenly started getting frenzied and got wrapped up in a cable. I'd been temporarily distracted and turned around to see his paw wrapped around a white cable. He was pulling on it and was threatening to drag one of the giant consoles with him.

'Oh God, Bob, what are you doing?' I said.

I'd not been the only one to spot this. A couple of Apple 'geniuses' were standing there laughing.

'He's a star, isn't he?' one of them said.

Unfortunately, they were soon joined by another, more senior member of the team.

'If he breaks anything, I'm afraid you'd have to cover the costs,' he said. Given the prices of the products on display in the store, I wasted no time in untangling him and getting the hell out of there.

For Bob, London is an endless source of opportunities to get up to no good. Even the underground has become a place where he can misbehave.

When we first got together he would cling to me closely whenever we travelled underground. He didn't like going down the escalators and lifts and felt intimidated by the crowds and the claustrophobic atmosphere during the rush hour. Over the years, however, he has conquered his fears. He even has his own identity card, given to him by the staff at Angel tube station and behaves just like any other Londoner, going about his or her business. He trots along the tunnels, always walking as near to the wall as possible, probably for security. When we get to the platform, he stands behind the yellow line, unflustered when the train pulls into the station, despite the noise it makes. He waits for it to go past him, then waits patiently for the doors to slide open before padding quietly on board and checking for an empty seat.

Londoners are notorious for not engaging with their fellow commuters, but even the most ice-hearted melt a little when they see him sitting there, studiously taking in the atmosphere. They snap away with their camera phones then head off to work smiling. Living in London can be such an impersonal and soul-destroying existence. The idea that we are somehow lightening people's days makes me smile.

Travelling on the tube has its perils, however.

One evening we'd headed home from central London and got the tube to Seven Sisters, the nearest tube station to my flat. There was a lot of maintenance and repair work being done within the tube at the time and Bob had been fascinated by the various bits of equipment and heavy-duty gear that was visible here and there.

It was as we were coming up the escalator that I noticed Bob's tail was sticky. When I looked at it a little closer, I could see some sort of black, tar-like material on his tail. I then saw that it was also streaked along his body, from the middle of his ribcage back to halfway along his tail.

It was pretty obvious he'd rubbed up against something during his ride on the tube because it wasn't there beforehand. I was at a loss to know what it was exactly. It looked like engine oil or some sort of heavy grease. It definitely looked like it had come from something mechanical. I guessed he must have rubbed up against some of the engineering equipment somehow.

The one thing I did know was that it was potentially harmful. Bob seemed to have worked this out as well. I saw that he'd spotted the mess and had already decided that giving it a lick wasn't a good idea.

My phone was low on credit but I had just about enough to make a call and rang a friend, Rosemary, a vet who had helped us out once before when Bob had been ill. She loved Bob and was always willing to help. When I explained what had happened she told me that whatever it was I needed to get it washed off.

'Motor and engine oil can be highly toxic to cats, especially if it's ingested or inhaled. It can cause really bad inflammation and burning of organs, especially the lungs. It can also cause breathing problems, seizure and even death in really bad cases,' she said, scaring me. 'So you really need to wash it off him. Does Bob let you bathe him?' she said. 'If it doesn't come off, you should take him to the Blue Cross or another vet first thing in the morning,' she said just before I ran out of credit and my phone cut out.

Cats seem to fall into two categories when it comes to bath time: there are those who hate it and those that love it. Luckily, Bob falls well and truly into the second camp. In fact, he is a bit obsessed with his bath.

He loves nothing more than climbing into the tub when I run a bath. He has learned that I always run a warm bath rather than a steaming hot one and hops into the tub so that he can paddle around in it for a few minutes.

It is funny – and, of course, very cute – to watch him walking around afterwards as he lifts and shakes one paw at a time.

He also gets very possessive about the bath plug and steals and hides it. I end up using a makeshift plug only to find the real plug lying on the living room floor where Bob has been playing with it.

Sometimes I have to put a jug with a weight on it over the plug to stop him from stealing and hiding it.

So given all that it was no problem getting him into the bath so that I could get this mystery grease off his tail.

I didn't have to hold him down. I used both

hands to rub his tail and his side using some cat-friendly shower gel. I then hosed him down with the shower head. The expression on his face as the jets of water soaked into his body was hilarious, a mix of a grimace and a grin. Finally I dried him off as best I could with a towel. Again he didn't need much persuasion to be rubbed down. He loved it and was purring throughout.

I managed to get all of the nasty stuff off him. But there was still a faint stain on his tail and body. Over the next few days, however, he was able to lick it and it slowly began to disappear. I popped into the Blue Cross at Islington later that week and got them to give him a quick check up. They told me there was nothing to worry about.

'Easier said than done, there's always something to fret about with this one,' I said to the nurse, realising afterwards that I'd actually begun to sound a little like a parent.

The incident on the tube reminded me of a truth that I always kept in my mind. In the years since we'd found each other, I'd domesticated Bob to a certain degree. When it came down to it though, he remained a stray cat at heart.

I can't be 100 per cent certain, but my gut feeling

is that he must have spent a large part of his young life living off his wits on the streets. He is a Londoner, born and bred, and is never happier than when he is exploring it. I often smile to myself and say '*you can take the cat out of the street, but you can't take the street out of the cat*'.

He has a few favourite haunts. At Angel, he loves visiting Islington Memorial Green, the little park where he is free to rummage around in the bushes, sniffing out whatever caught his interest while he did his business. There are a few overgrown corners where he can discreetly disappear for a few moments of privacy. Not that privacy bothers him too much.

He is also, for instance, very fond of the grounds of St Giles in the Fields churchyard just off Tottenham Court Road. Often, when we walk from our bus stop on Tottenham Court Road towards Neal Street and Covent Garden, he starts moving around on my shoulder letting me know that he wants to make it a port of call.

The graveyard at St Giles is an oasis in the middle of one of the busiest parts of the city, with benches to sit and watch the world go by. For some reason, however, Bob's favourite toilet spot there is actually in full view of the street, by a set of railings on a wall. He is unfazed by the flood of Londoners passing by and quietly goes about his business there.

It was a similar story when we were working on Neal Street where his preferred option was outside an office block on Endell Street. It was overlooked by several floors of conference rooms and offices, so again, wasn't exactly the most private spot in London. But Bob felt comfortable there and always managed to squeeze himself into the shrubbery so that he could get on with things as quickly and efficiently as possible.

Wherever he goes, he is, like all cats, very methodical about it. He digs himself a decent-sized hole, places himself over it while he does the necessary, then starts scrabbling dirt to cover up the evidence afterwards. He is always meticulous in levelling it all off so that no one would know it was there. It always fascinates me to know why cats do this. I read somewhere that it's a territorial thing.

The gardens in Soho Square were another favourite stop-off if we were working in that area. Apart from being one of the most beautiful little parks in central London, it had other attractions for Bob. Dogs were banned, for instance, which meant I could relax a little more if I let Bob off the leash. It was also a place where Bob seemed happy, especially in the summer. Bob was fascinated by birds and Soho Square park was filled with them. He would sit there, wide-eyed, staring at them, making a curious little noise, a sort of *raa, raa, raa*. It sounded really cute, although, in reality of

course, it was probably quite siniste
where that scientists think cats mimic
they see potential prey. In other word
practising chomping them to bits in th
when they catch them.

That made sense. Bob loves nothing more than
chasing mice and rats and other creatures when let
loose in parks. On several occasions, he'd wandered
over to me with something he'd found – and probably killed – while he was roaming around.

One day, I was reading a comic book in Soho
Square when he arrived with something absolutely
disgusting dangling from his mouth. It was part of
a rat's head.

'Bob, that's going to make you really sick,' I said.

He seemed to know this better than me. I don't
think he had any intention of eating it. Instead he
took it into a corner and started playing with it,
much like he played with his scraggedy mouse at
home. Ninety nine times out of a hundred Bob
drew admiring glances from passers-by. On that
particular occasion, a few people looked at him in
utter horror.

I had never been one of those cat owners who
saw their pets as little angels, incapable of doing
anything nasty. Far from it. I knew all too well that,
like all members of his species, Bob was a predator
and a highly effective one at that. If we had been
living in other parts of the world, I'd have been

re concerned. In parts of the USA, Australia and New Zealand, in particular, they have tried to introduce bans on cats being allowed out after dark. They claim domestic cats are doing so much damage that birdlife in particular is being endangered. That wasn't a problem in London. So, as far as I was concerned, Bob was free to do what came naturally to him. As long as he didn't risk hurting or harming himself.

Apart from anything else, it is great entertainment, for him – and for me.

One day, for instance, we were looking after Titch's dog Princess again and I'd decided to take the pair of them to a small park near the flats where I live. It's not the most glamorous green space in London. It's got a rundown basketball court and a tree-lined area. But that was enough for them.

I was sitting on a bench with Bob on the extralong lead I'd made for him when he suddenly spotted a grey squirrel.

Princess spotted it too and soon the pair of them were bounding towards it. The squirrel, quite sensibly, scampered up the nearest tree, but Bob and Princess weren't deterred.

I watched them as they worked together trying to work out how to flush the squirrel out of the tree. It was like watching a SWAT team trying to winkle a bad guy out of a safe house.

Princess would let out a bark every now and again to try and rattle the squirrel. Every time the squirrel appeared or made a move, the two would adjust their positions. Bob was covering one side, leading back on to the open space towards me, while Princess was covering the squirrel's other potential escape route at the back of the tree.

They carried on with this for twenty minutes before eventually giving up.

I'm sure some people must have thought that I was ever-so-slightly mad. But I sat there grinning and giggling away, engrossed by every captivating minute of it.

Chapter 13

Public Enemy No 1

Another summer was on its way and the midday sun was already blazing as Bob and I settled ourselves in a shady spot outside Angel tube station. I had just got out a bowl and filled it with some water for Bob when I saw two men approaching.

They were both dressed casually, in jeans and jumpers. One was in his late twenties while the other was, I guessed, a decade or so older, probably in his late thirties. Almost in unison, they produced badges from their pockets showing they were police officers, members of the CSU, Community Safety Unit for Islington.

'Hello there, Sir. Can you tell me your name?' the older of them asked me.

'Erm, it's James Bowen, why?'

'Mr Bowen, I'm afraid we have had an allegation of assault made against you. It's a serious matter so we are going to have to ask you to accompany us to the police station to answer a few questions,' the younger guy said.

Plain-clothes policemen were a fairly frequent fixture on the streets and I'd encountered my fair share of them. Fortunately, unlike some of their colleagues, who could be a little aggressive and anti-*Big Issue* vendors, these two were perfectly polite.

When I asked if I could take a minute to pack up my pitch and sort Bob out, they told me to take as much time as I wanted. They then told me that we were going to walk towards their HQ at Tolpuddle Street.

'Shouldn't take us more than a few minutes,' the younger officer said.

I was surprised at how calm I was. In the past I'd have started panicking and would probably have protested, possibly even violently. It was a measure of how much more controlled and together I was these days. Besides, I hadn't done anything. I hadn't assaulted anyone.

The police officers seemed pretty chilled too. As we made our way to the station, they were walking along quite happily in front of me and Bob. Occasionally one would drop back to walk with us. At one point, the younger of the two asked me whether I understood what was happening and whether I knew my rights.

'Yeah, sure,' I said.

I knew I hadn't been charged with anything and that I was just helping them with their enquiries. There was no need to call a lawyer or anything like that, at this stage at least.

Obviously, my mind was churning away, trying to work out who might have made this 'allegation'. I had a few thoughts already.

The most obvious explanation was that this was someone just trying to muck up my day. Sadly, it was pretty common. I'd seen it happen to other vendors and buskers over the years. Someone with a grudge or just an evil streak would make an accusation which the police would be obliged to check out. Sometimes they'd do it simply to get the person away from their pitch and then claim it for themselves. There were a few people around who, I knew, didn't like the fact that I'd made the tube pitch a success and would love to have taken it over. It was nasty, but it was a fact of life, unfortunately.

The other, more sinister, possibility, was that it was someone trying to undermine my book. By now pretty much everyone in *The Big Issue* community knew about it. More newspapers had picked up on the story and several vendors had made comments, positive and negative.

I'd been told by one of the co-ordinators that someone had been putting it around that I shouldn't be allowed to sell the magazine any more. I knew this already because one vendor in central London had made his objections plain and to my face. He had also called me 'a f***ing hippy poser', which was rather charming I thought. Stupidly, I'd imagined that I was doing something positive for the magazine. Instead, it felt at times like I'd turned into every vendor's Public Enemy No 1.

By the time we got to the station both of the police officers were on first name terms with Bob. They seemed really smitten with him, so much so that he was their first priority when we arrived at the station.

'Right let's get Bob settled before we take you into the custody suite,' the older officer said.

We were soon joined by a blonde, uniformed female PC in her late twenties. She immediately focussed on Bob, who was still wrapped around my shoulders, trying to take in the unfamiliar scenery.

'OK, is this Bob?' she said, reaching up to him and giving him a stroke. He seemed to take an instant shine to her and was soon rubbing his face on her hand, purring away as he did so.

'Do you think he'd mind if I picked him up?' she said.

'Sure, if he will come to you then go for it,' I said, sensing that he was already really at ease with her.

As I suspected, he let her scoop him up.

'Why don't you come with me and we can see if

we can sort you out with something nice to eat or drink?' she said.

I watched as they headed behind the main reception desk to an office area with desks and photocopiers and fax machines. Bob was fascinated by all the red lights and buzzing machines and was happy in there. So I left him there as I headed off with the officers.

'Don't worry, he's safe with Gillian,' the younger officer said to me as we went through a set of doors into the custody suite. I felt certain he was telling the truth.

As we headed into an interview room, I suddenly felt butterflies in my stomach. It had been explained to me that I was being questioned about one of the so-called 'trigger offences'. These were offences in which drug users or dealers committed crimes like shoplifting, robbery and assault in order to buy drugs. So as a result of this, I knew that I would probably need to be tested for drugs as well as fingerprinted.

How times had changed? A year or so earlier and I'd have been seriously concerned about this. But now I had no qualms at all as they conducted the so-called Cozart test and swabbed my mouth for traces of heroin or cocaine. I knew I was clean. I told the officers this but they said they had no option.

'It's regulation now I'm afraid,' one of them said.

Once that was over, they sat me down and asked me some questions.

They asked me whether I'd been in a location somewhere in Islington a day earlier. The address didn't sound at all familiar. They then mentioned the name of a woman.

Years earlier, at the depths of my drug addiction, when I'd been arrested a couple of times for shoplifting I'd learned to simply answer 'no comment' to any questions like this. But I knew this was really irritating for the police, so I tried to be co-operative.

'I'd like to help you, but I honestly don't know what you are talking about,' I said.

They didn't get angry or pushy in their questioning at all. There was no 'good cop, bad cop' routine. They just nodded at my answers, took down some notes and that was it. After about ten minutes, or less, we were done.

'OK, Mr Bowen, well we need you to stay here for a bit while we look into this further,' the younger officer said.

By now it had turned into a very bright, sunny afternoon outside. I was impatient to be reunited with Bob and to get back to work. But the clock kept ticking and before I knew it the shadows were lengthening. It was really frustrating and I was also worried about Bob. At one stage a duty PC offered me a cup of tea so I asked about him.

'It's OK, he's with Gillian still downstairs,' he said. 'Think she's been out to get him some treats, so he's a pretty happy chappie down there.'

Eventually, the two officers who'd first approached me, came back into the interview room.

'I'm afraid I think we've wasted your time and our time,' they said. 'The person who made this accusation on the phone hasn't been willing to come down to give a formal statement. So there's no corroborating evidence against you and so there will be no charges.'

I was obviously relieved. I felt angry as well, but decided to bottle it up. There was no point in making a formal complaint or threatening legal action, especially as everyone had been so decent. It was best to just get the hell out of there and get back to work.

My main concern, once more was Bob. What had they done with him for all this time?

I had to go down to the reception area to sign out. Bob was there with Gillian, looking as content as when I'd left him. But the moment he saw me his tail started swishing and his ears perked up. He leapt into my arms.

'Gosh, someone's pleased to see you,' Gillian said.

'Has he been a good boy?' I asked her.

'He's been a star. Haven't you, Bob?' she said.

I saw that she had set him up in a corner of her

office. She told me that she'd been out to the shops and bought him some cat milk, a pouch of meaty food and an enormous packet of his favourite treats. No wonder he was so happy, I thought.

We chatted for a moment or two while they got my bag and tabard from wherever it had been put during my interview upstairs. Gillian told me in normal circumstances he'd have been placed with any stray dogs that were being held.

'If you'd been kept in overnight we'd have had to think about putting him there,' she said. 'But luckily that won't be necessary now.'

I'd soon been officially released. The two officers were apologetic again.

'Just someone being spiteful I guess,' I said to them, shaking their hands as I left.

By the time I had left the station it was getting towards sunset. All day I'd been paranoid that someone had stolen my pitch so I headed back to Angel just to check. To my relief, there was no one there.

'You all right, James?' one of the flower sellers asked me.

'Yeah, just someone's idea of a joke. Reporting me for assault.'

'Really? What's wrong with people?' he said, shaking his head in disgust.

It was a good question, one to which I had absolutely no answer unfortunately.

Around a week to ten days later, Bob and I were selling magazines during the rush hour, when an attractive, blonde lady came up to us. Bob seemed to recognise her and arched his head towards her when she knelt down beside him.

'You don't remember me, do you?' she said to me as she made a fuss of him.

So many faces were flashing past us each night outside the tube, it was hard to register everyone. She could obviously see I was struggling.

"Tolpuddle Street station? I was the one who looked after Bob the other week,' she smiled.

'Oh, yes, of course. Sorry,' I said, genuinely mortified. 'It's Gillian, isn't it?'

'Looks like you are both doing well,' she said.

Community police officers had stopped to talk to us over the years, but she didn't seem to be 'on duty'. She wasn't in uniform for a start.

'On my way home from the end of my shift,' she said, when I mentioned this.

'We didn't really have much of a chance to talk when you were at the station the other day, for obvious reasons,' Gillian said. 'So how did you two get together?'

She smiled and laughed out loud a couple of times as I recounted our early days together.

'Soul mates by the sound of it,' she said.

She could tell that I was busy and that the rush hour was about to begin, so was soon on her way.

'I might pop in and see you again if that's all right,' she said.

'Sure,' I said.

She was true to her word and was soon stopping by to see us regularly, often bringing gifts for Bob. He seemed to have a genuine soft spot for her.

Gillian was generous to me as well. On one occasion she brought me a coffee, a sandwich and a cookie from one of the smart local sandwich bars. We chatted for a little while, both of us skirting around what had happened at the station a few weeks earlier. A part of me was curious to find out who had made this allegation against me, but I knew she couldn't go into too much detail. It would have been too risky for her.

I explained to her what was happening to us with the book and how it seemed to have generated more animosity than anything else.

'Ah don't worry about that. People are always jealous of other's success. It sounds great,' she said. 'Your friends and family must be so proud of you.'

'Yeah, they are,' I said, giving her a sheepish smile and lighting up a cigarette.

Of course, the truth was that I didn't have too many friends. Aside from Belle, there was no one to whom I could turn – in the good times or the bad times. I had Bob and that was about it.

It was, in part, the life that I'd made for myself. I was a product of the environment in which I'd spent the past decade.

When I'd been on drugs I'd withdrawn from the world. My most important relationships back then were with my dealers. But even now that I was clean, I found it hard to establish friendships. There were several reasons. Money, for a start. To make friends you had to go out and socialise, which cost money so I very rarely did that. But on a deeper level, I also found it hard to trust people. During the worst period of my drug dependency, I'd stayed in hostels where you knew that anyone could rob you of all your possessions any moment. Even when you were asleep. So I'd become very wary. It was sad, but I still felt that way to a large extent. The events of the past couple of weeks had underlined that. Someone had made a fictitious assault accusation against me. For all I knew it could have been someone I saw every day of the week. It could have been someone I regarded as a 'friend'.

So as I looked at Bob interacting with Gillian, a part of me wished my life could be as simple and straightforward as his. He had met her in strange circumstances but had immediately sensed he could trust her. He knew in his bones that she was a decent person and so he had embraced her as a friend. I knew it wasn't going to be easy, but I needed to do that more. I needed to take that same leap of faith. To do that, however, I had to change my life. I had to get off the streets.

Chapter 14

Pride and Prejudice

It was the first Saturday of July and the streets of central London were packed for the annual Gay Pride celebrations. The West End was a sea of colour – well mostly pink – as the hot weather had drawn even more revellers than usual. According to the news, a million people had ventured out on to the streets to watch the huge parade of floats, filled with drag queens, dancers and spectacular costumes snake its way from Oxford Circus, down Regent Street to Trafalgar Square.

I'd decided to kill two birds with one stone, and had spent the day watching the floats and fabulous outfits while also selling a few magazines at a pitch on Oxford Street near Oxford Circus tube station.

It was a lucrative day for all *The Big Issue* sellers so, as a 'visitor' from Islington, I had been careful to make sure I stayed within the rules. Some pitches, like my slot outside Angel tube station, are designated to only one authorised vendor but others, like this one, are free to anyone, provided there is no one else working there. I'd also been careful not to 'float', the term used to describe selling whilst walking around the streets. I'd fallen foul of that rule in the past and didn't want to do so again.

During the decade or so that I had been on the streets, Gay Pride had grown from a small, quite political march into one of the city's biggest street parties. Only the Notting Hill Carnival was bigger. This year the crowds were packed four or five deep in places, but everyone was in an incredibly good mood, including Bob.

He'd got used to being in big crowds. There had been a time when he had a slight phobia of people in really scary outfits. He'd run off years earlier after seeing a guy in a weird, over-sized suit outside Ripley's Believe It Or Not in Piccadilly Circus. His years of walking the streets of London and Covent Garden in particular, seemed to have eased his fears, however. He'd seen everything from weird, silver-painted human statues to French fire-eaters to giant dragons during Chinese New Year. Today, there was no shortage of outrageous outfits and people blowing horns and whistles but he took it all in his stride. He sat on my shoulder throughout, soaking the party atmosphere up and loving the attention he was getting from the huge crowds. Quite a few people knew him by name and asked to have their picture taken with the pair of us. One or two even said they were looking forward to reading about us in our book.

'We need to write it first,' I half-joked.

As the main parade drew to an end late in the afternoon, Bob and I headed towards Soho Square where there was a music stage and some other events and turned into Old Compton Street, home to many of London's most popular gay bars. The street was absolutely crammed full of people, many of them members of the procession who were now relaxing over a few drinks. About halfway along the street, I decided to have a cigarette. I didn't have a lighter on me so stopped at a table outside one of the pubs and asked to borrow one. To my surprise, a gay guy wearing nothing but a pair of pink Y-fronts, a pair of angel wings and a halo, produced one. I didn't want to think where he'd been keeping it.

'Here you go, mate. Nice cat by the way,' he said as he lit my cigarette for me.

I was still chatting to the guy when I felt a tap on my shoulder. I turned round to see an outreach worker called Holly. Judging by the way she was dressed in shorts and a t-shirt, I assumed she was off duty, mistakenly as it turned out.

'James. You're floating,' she said.

'No I'm not, Holly. I stopped to ask that guy for a light. Ask him if you like,' I said.

'You were floating, James. I saw you,' she said, adamant. 'I'm going to have to report you.'

I was gobsmacked.

'What? Oh, come on, Holly. You are going to report me for trying to get a light?' I protested, grabbing hold of the bag in which I now had only a couple of magazines left unsold. 'I'm done for the day. I didn't even have my magazines out.'

'Yeah, right,' she said, in a really sarcastic tone before sliding off into the crowd.

I wasn't sure whether to take her threat seriously or not. Every outreach worker was different. Some carried through on their threats, others made them purely to make a point. I decided that she wasn't going to spoil my day and carried on enjoying the party atmosphere.

I took the Sunday off and went back to work on Monday, as normal. By then I'd forgotten completely about Holly. It was on Wednesday that the trouble began.

Arriving in Islington just before midday, I went to see Rita, the co-ordinator on Islington Green to buy new supplies of magazines.

'Sorry, James, I can't sell you any. You are on the "To Be Seen" list,' she said.

'What?!'

'Apparently someone saw you floating in the West End. You know the drill. You've got to go over to Head Office in Vauxhall.'

'Bloody Holly,' I said to myself.

It was infuriating for all sorts of reasons. First and foremost, of course, it was a complete nonsense to say I'd been floating. I'd had this problem before, mainly because so many people approached me and Bob when we were walking around London.

I knew I wasn't supposed to sell magazines when on the move. I could only do so from a fixed pitch. I'd always tried to explain this to people and, whilst some were confused and even offended, they usually moved along without giving me anything. Unfortunately, all it needed was for another *Big Issue* seller or an outreach worker to see me having any kind of exchange with a member of the public and they'd put two and two together to make five.

It was a real bore having to travel over to Vauxhall, but I knew I had to keep my pitch at Angel going. The book was just a passing phase, I knew I couldn't turn my back on what was still my bread and butter.

At *The Big Issue* office, I had to sit around for half an hour before I could see a supervisor. When I eventually got called in, this guy told me that I had been mentioned at the weekly outreach worker meeting where they discuss pitch disputes, misbehaving vendors and other issues.

'I'm afraid you are going to have to serve a one month suspension because an outreach worker saw you table-top floating,' he said.

I tried to defend myself. But it was a waste of breath. With *The Big Issue* you were guilty unless you formally appealed. I'd been through that process before, when I'd been based in Covent Garden. Again, I'd been unfairly accused of floating and it had come down to my word against theirs. My word apparently wasn't worth much and I'd lost.

I knew it was pointless appealing this time so I decided to take it on the chin and accept the suspension. I signed the relevant paperwork, handed in my tabard and ID card and headed home, upset but resigned to the fact that this was the way the cookie crumbled.

'What's that saying? No good deed goes unpunished,' I said to Bob as we sat on the tube heading back home.

I figured that, with the book still to be written, I would spend the month working on that, doing a little busking and return to Angel tube station in a month's time. If only it had been that simple.

At the end of the month, I went back to *The Big Issue* office. I wasn't certain that I'd get my tabard and ID back that day so took my guitar with me, in case I needed to carry on busking. I needn't have worried. I was told I had served my 'sentence' and got my stuff back. I also bought a supply of magazines to take back to Angel.

'Back to business, Bob,' I said as we caught a bus and headed back across the Thames.

Arriving back at Angel, I emerged from the station and saw my pitch was empty. It was still registered to me, so no one else should technically have been there although I wouldn't have been surprised if someone had chanced it. So I set up as normal and got back to work.

I'd been there for about half an hour when another vendor arrived. He was a guy I'd seen around occasionally. He was relatively new to *The Big Issue* and had a rather scruffy and bad-tempered old dog.

'What are you doing? This is my pitch' he said.

'No it's not,' I said, looking bemused. 'This has been my pitch for more than a year now.'

'It might have been your pitch a year ago, but it's mine now. I'm registered with head office.'

'What? I really don't know what you're on about, mate. Bob and I are part of the furniture here. They've even written about us in the newspapers,' I said, trying to remain reasonable.

He just shrugged his shoulders and blew out his cheeks.

'What can I say?' he muttered. 'Go and talk to Rita. She'll fill you in.'

'I will, mate, don't you worry about that,' I said,

marching straight across the High Street towards the co-ordinator's spot on Islington Green.

It was obvious immediately that something was wrong because Rita's face crumpled when she saw me.

'Oh, hi, James,' she said, refusing to make eye contact.

'Look. It wasn't my decision. I told him it was your pitch and that you were on a month's suspension. He stayed away for a fortnight but then he went down to Vauxhall and someone there went over my head. They told him he could have it full time. There was nothing I could do.'

I was stunned. For a moment I was lost for words.

It may sound boastful, but I had turned that pitch into a money-spinner for *The Big Issue*, and myself, obviously. Until I had arrived there, no one had wanted to work there. The conventional wisdom had always been that people were in too much of a hurry to slow down at that spot. They didn't have time to engage with a vendor. But, largely thanks to Bob, of course, I had established myself there. Even the outreach workers had said that the number of people who came to see us was amazing. As were sales of the magazine.

'I can't believe they've done this to me,' I said to Rita, scrambling to work out why this had happened. 'Is it because I've got this book deal and they assume

I don't need to sell any more?' I said. 'Because if it is they've got it all wrong. That's only a flash in the pan. I need to keep working long term.'

But Rita wasn't responding. She just kept shaking her head and saying 'I don't know' or 'I'm sorry'.

In the end I just stormed off, with Bob on my shoulders.

Looking back, I am not proud of what I did next, but I felt so cheated and badly treated that I decided to take matters into my own hands.

I headed back to the tube station and confronted the guy again.

'Look mate, here's £20 for the pitch. How's that?' I said.

He pondered it for a moment then grabbed the note, picked up his magazines and headed off with his dog in tow. I had barely been there ten minutes when he arrived back, this time with Holly in tow.

'James, this isn't your pitch any more,' she said.

'Yes, it is. I just paid the guy £20 to get it back,' I said.

'It doesn't work that way and you know it, James,' she said.

My head was spinning now. I couldn't understand why they were doing this to me. Had I behaved so badly? Was I that unpopular amongst *The Big Issue* fraternity? I must have been. They all seemed to have it in for me.

'So can I have my £20 back?' I said to the guy.

'No. I haven't earned anything yet,' he said.

I could see that he hadn't bought any magazines, so he couldn't have spent the £20. I lost it this time and started busking about twenty feet away from my usual pitch.

'James, what are you doing?' Holly said. I just ignored her and played on.

She slipped away briefly but reappeared with a police officer and another outreach worker, John, in tow.

'I'm afraid I'm going to have to ask you to move on, Sir. Otherwise I will have no option but to caution you,' the PC said.

'James you are also going to have to hand in your tabard and your ID,' Holly said. 'You are going to get another suspension for this.'

I'd only got them back a couple of hours earlier. But I handed them over.

This time I knew *The Big Issue* were going to be even harsher in their punishment, and I'd be given a six month suspension. I decided that enough was enough. I decided that I would end my association with them. I didn't feel great about it. Selling the magazine had done wonders for me. But I just felt a deep sense of injustice.

I wasn't an angel. To be honest, I don't think anyone who sells *The Big Issue* really is. We've all got our faults. We wouldn't be working on the streets if we didn't, would we? I also realised that I had probably over-reacted and lost my temper when I'd discovered my pitch had been given away. I just felt betrayed, especially because Bob and I had become unofficial ambassadors for the magazine. After we'd gone on the first Night Walk, we'd effectively been the public faces of the event and had featured in a lot of the publicity for a second one that had taken place. By this point I'd also been in the *Islington Tribune* a couple of times and the *Camden Journal*. The *Independent* had even published a piece. Each and every one of them mentioned that I was selling *The Big Issue*. It was the kind of feel-good coverage they wanted. We embodied the ethos of the charity: they had helped us to help ourselves. Or at least, so I thought.

I began to wonder whether they saw it differently. Maybe they thought I was getting too big for my boots. I actually dug out my original contract with them to see if I'd perhaps broken any rules by agreeing to write a book. But, perhaps surprisingly, there was nothing. *The Big Issue* sellers obviously didn't generally get contracts with big publishers to write their stories.

It was really confusing. I really didn't know what to think. Once again, I began to wonder whether the high profile Bob and I were winning was a double-edged sword. But I knew what I had to do.

I didn't go to Vauxhall to sign my six month

suspension. As far as I was concerned, I'd sold my last copy of the magazine. I was sick of all the politics and the back-stabbing. It was bringing out the worst in people – but more worryingly, it was bringing out the worst in me. From now on I needed to concentrate on Bob, the book and all the things that brought out the best in me.

Chapter 15

The One That Saves Me

The drama at Angel left me feeling depressed and lost for a little while. Deep down I knew I'd done the right thing, but I still had my moments when I worried that I'd made a bad move. I fretted that I'd made an enemy of *The Big Issue* and that it might come back to bite me somehow.

It took me a week or so to snap out of it. I gave myself a talking-to. I told myself that I couldn't dwell on it forever. I had to move on and, in particular, I had to focus on the positives, especially the book.

It had been delivered to the publishers who seemed pleased with it. A part of me had wondered whether they'd read it and get cold feet. My story wasn't the most romantic or glamorous of tales. The life on the streets I'd described was grim and, at times, deeply unpleasant. For a week or two after Garry and I handed in the manuscript, I half expected a phone call saying 'sorry, we've made a

221

terrible mistake'. But that didn't happen. Instead they told me they were going to publish it in the following spring, in March.

I now had a target to aim for, but in the meantime I had to keep earning money, so I headed back to busking – and to Covent Garden.

I had mixed feelings. On the negative side, after a couple of years selling *The Big Issue*, it felt like a little bit of a backward step. Busking is, in some ways, only one rung up from begging. I thought I'd put those days behind me.

The other problem was that my voice had deteriorated. Shouting out 'Big Issue, Big Issue' hundreds and hundreds of times a day was more demanding on the larynx than singing a tuneful song every now and again. So when I picked up my guitar and started singing again I felt that I was well below par, certainly from the previous time I'd been performing. Playing the guitar for long periods took some getting used to as well. I didn't have callouses on my fingers for a start.

They were the negatives, but there were some positives too. I tried to focus on them.

Most significantly, it was a step into independence. *The Big Issue* had, without question, been a force for good in my life. Its guiding mantra had always been that it offered a helping hand rather than hand-outs. That had certainly been true in my case. It had helped me bring a little stability to my life. Without them I would probably never have been asked to write a book.

Yes, I'd found it hard to abide by the rules of an organisation. Some of it was bad luck, some of it was down to personality clashes, but some of it – I had to hold my hands up – was down to me. I wasn't very good at dealing with authority. I never had been.

So being my own person again, felt good. I felt I'd got my freedom back.

Of course, the other really positive thing was that Bob and I were better known now. Thanks to the various pieces in newspapers and on the internet, we were minor local celebrities.

From the first day busking, it was clear to me that we were now drawing bigger crowds than previously. There would be times when little semi-circles of tourists and shoppers would surround us, snapping away with their cameras and kneeling down to stroke Bob. I was shocked at how many people speaking foreign languages that I didn't even recognise would smile, point and say: 'Aaaah, Bob.'

Bob seemed to relish it. One of the most requested songs I played was 'Wonderwall' by Oasis. It was an easy song to play. I just put a capo on the second fret of my guitar and started strumming away. I'd played it a hundred times, but now, each time I played those familiar chords, the lyrics hit home much harder, in particular that line in the chorus that goes: *'Maybe you're gonna be the one that saves me'*. As I looked down at Bob, I realised it could have been written for him. There was no maybe about it. He had saved me.

Another positive about being in Covent Garden, of course, was that life was never, ever dull there. I soon remembered that the place had a rhythm and life all of its own. The busiest time of the day was the evening rush, around 7pm, when hordes of people headed home from work and an even bigger horde flooded in to visit the bars, restaurants, theatres and opera houses.

Watching the world go by from our position on Neal Street, it was never difficult to spot who was headed where. You could spot the kids who were out for a night's clubbing a mile away. They were all mini-skirts and towering heels, leather jackets and hair gel. The opera lovers were generally the best dressed, often with the men in black tie and the women in grand evening dresses with a generous helping of bling thrown in for good measure. You could hear some of them rattling down the road in the direction of the Piazza and the Royal Opera House. The area was full of characters. As we settled back into the routine, we seemed to attract more than our fair share of them once more.

One afternoon, a couple of weeks into summer, I noticed an unfamiliar face on the pavement a few yards away from us.

It wasn't uncommon for other people to set up in the area, trying to earn a few quid. I didn't have any problem with that, as long as they didn't interfere with our livelihood. The only rivals who really annoyed me were 'chuggers', the freelance charity workers who would swarm around an area from time to time, pestering people.

I wasn't being hypocritical. We all had a living to earn, and I had been a bit pushy myself when I was selling *The Big Issue*. But the chuggers took things too far and their behaviour could be so downright rude and intrusive it was bordering on harassment.

This guy was definitely not one of them, however. He was dark skinned and dressed quite smartly, in a suit. He had an odd-looking basket, which he placed on the floor. I guessed he was some kind of street entertainer, but I had no idea what to expect.

I was intrigued and sat there watching him for a few moments, hoping he might ease the boredom of another day. I wasn't disappointed. He had soon dipped into his basket and produced a yellowish snake which he then proceeded to drape around his neck. I was no expert on snakes, but I'd have described it as an albino python. It was quite thick and about three feet long. He then started playing around with it, asking for donations from passers-by.

'Look Bob, we've got a snake charmer,' I smiled as I watched the impressive-looking creature coiling its way around the guy.

Bob was weighing up the situation carefully, but it was obvious he didn't really understand what was happening. We were a good thirty feet away so he couldn't really see properly, so he settled back into his favourite position in the shade and started his afternoon snooze.

The guy had been there for about forty minutes or so when he came over to say hello. He still had the snake draped on his neck as if it was a rather large piece of jewellery.

'OK, guys, how are you today?' he said, in a strong accent that I guessed was Portuguese or possibly Brazilian.

Bob had been dozing away in the afternoon sun but perked up and took a good look at the curious visitor. I could tell his mind was hard at work, trying to work out what this creature was – and whether it was a welcome presence in his world? It didn't take him long to reach his conclusion.

As Bob tilted his head forward to take a better look, the snake decided to stick out its long, forked tongue and deliver a rather scary hiss. It was like something out of *The Jungle Book*.

Bob completely freaked. He made this really loud, yowling sound and jumped up at me imploring me to stick him on my shoulders. I was pretty sure that if I hadn't had his harness connected to me he would have bolted and run off, as he'd done once over in Angel, when an aggressive dog had lunged at him.

'Sorry, dude, didn't mean to scare your cat,' the guy said, realising what he'd done and sliding the snake off his shoulders. 'I'm going to move away from here and see how I get on further down the road.'

Bob spent the rest of the afternoon on edge. He was so paranoid about meeting another snake that he kept attacking the straps on my rucksack. He'd been sitting on this rucksack for years and had never had a problem. But suddenly anything that reminded him of the yellow python was to be treated with extreme suspicion. He kept grabbing the straps in his teeth and flicking them in the air, as if to test whether they were alive or not.

It took Bob a few days to get over the snake. He was a little nervous whenever anyone came up to us in the street or elsewhere and kept checking out their shoulders as if he was worried there was someone lurking there. It must have been confusing for him. For all these years, he'd been the only creature that rode around the streets, draped across a man's neck. I think it completely threw him to see another creature there, especially such an alien and scary-looking one.

Of course it was all part of being back in the wacky world of Covent Garden.

Not everyone on the streets was so understanding. It remained a competitive and sometimes aggressive place, full of people only looking after No 1.

Bob and I were happily whiling away an afternoon on Neal Street when a young guy pitched up with an amplifier and a microphone. He was dressed in skater boy clothes and was wearing a baseball cap and Nike trainers. I spotted him setting up and waited for an instrument to appear, but there wasn't one. All he had was a microphone.

I ignored him and got back to playing my own music.

I wasn't able to shut him out of my mind for long though. Within minutes I heard an ear-splitting, repetitive noise booming out. The young guy was strutting around with his mic against his lips, 'beat boxing'. I'm a fan of most forms of music but this really wasn't my cup of tea. As far as I was concerned it wasn't remotely musical, it was just noise.

Bob shared my opinion, it was obvious. Maybe because he'd spent so long listening to me play acoustic guitar, he seemed to like that kind of music. He had also got used to slightly heavier rock. He made his opinion of this 'music' plain immediately. I looked down at him and saw him casting his eyes down the street with what I can only describe as complete disdain spread across his face.

There were times when I was led by Bob and this was one of them.

He stood up, tilted his head at me and let me know in no uncertain terms that we should move. I gathered my stuff and moved about 70 yards down the street where I began playing again. I could still hear the din from the young kid down the street, but at least I could hear myself think.

It was a false dawn.

The noise this kid was making was so loud that others must have complained because within half an hour or so a police van arrived. I watched from a distance as a couple of officers got out and approached him. I saw the boy waving his arms around in protest, but it didn't get him anywhere. A couple of minutes after the police's arrival I saw him disconnect his mike and start to pack up.

You could almost hear the sighs of relief that

must have been breathed in the offices, cafés and restaurants.

'Thank goodness that's over, eh Bob?' I said.

My joy was short-lived. The police officers saw Bob and me sitting on the pavement and came over to talk to us.

'You're not licensed to play here, mate,' one of them said.

I could have argued the toss and said we had a right to be there, which we kind of did. But I decided not to push it. Easing myself back into life in Covent Garden was difficult enough without aggravating the police. Choose your battles, James, I told myself, rather wisely, as it turned out.

It was just after midday on Neal Street and the crowds of tourists and shoppers were beginning to thicken. Bob and I had come out a little earlier today, partly because it was the first decent weather in a week but partly because we needed to get away by late afternoon so that I could get back home for a doctor's appointment.

I had developed a really bad chest problem and I'd had a week or so of sleepless nights coughing and wheezing. I had to get something done about it. I was getting really strung out by the lack of sleep.

I'd barely got myself set up and started playing when I saw a lady in a ribbed blue jumper and trousers walking purposefully towards me. I could tell she was not a tourist. As she drew close, I saw that her jumper had epaulettes and badges and had a familiar logo on it. She was from the RSPCA.

In ordinary circumstances, I was a big fan and supporter of the RSPCA. They do a great job in preventing animal cruelty and promoting animal welfare in general and had been a huge help to me in the past. When I'd first found Bob injured in the hallway of my block of flats I'd taken him to a nearby drop-in clinic. As well as giving me a prescription for the medicine Bob would need to heal his wounds, the vet there had passed on lots of sound and sensible advice on how to treat and care for him.

That now seemed like a very distant memory. Today, I got the distinct impression that their presence wasn't going to be good news.

'Hello, James, how are you today?' the lady said, producing a card with her ID on it. It showed that she was an Inspector.

I was a bit thrown by the fact that she knew my name.

'Fine, thanks. What's the problem?'

'I've been asked to come and see you because I'm afraid we have had complaints that you are mistreating your cat, Bob isn't it?' she said.

'What?! Mistreating him? How?'

I was horrified. My head was spinning. Who had complained? And what had they said I was doing to Bob? I felt physically sick for a moment, but knew I had to keep my wits about me in case this got serious.

'I'm sure they are unfounded allegations. I was actually watching you for a little while before I came over and I can see that you treat Bob well,' she said, giving him a little tickle under the chin. 'But I do need to have a chat with you and then examine him to make sure there's nothing wrong if that's OK.'

'Be my guest,' I said, knowing that I didn't really have a choice.

She dropped her rucksack to the floor, got out a notebook and a couple of instruments and kneeled down to start examining Bob.

He didn't always take kindly to people poking and prodding him. He had reacted to a couple of vets over the years and had snarled and scratched at one nurse who had handled him a bit roughly once. So I was a bit concerned about how he'd react to this latest stranger, especially if he picked up on my nervousness. That was all I needed, I thought to myself.

It wasn't the first time people had accused me of mistreating him, of course. I'd heard all sorts of accusations levelled against me. The complaints generally fell into three categories. The first was that I was exploiting and 'using' him for my own benefit. My answer to that argument was always the same. As someone once said, a cat will be your friend, but it will never be your slave. A cat is never, ever going to do something it doesn't want to do. And it is never going to be with someone it doesn't want to be with, no matter what that person does to it. Bob was a very strong character, with a free will of his own. He wouldn't have hung around if he didn't trust and like me. And it was his choice whether he wanted to come out with me each day.

There were still days when he didn't fancy taking to the streets. They were rare, to be honest. He genuinely enjoyed being out and about, meeting people and being fussed over. But when he hid away or refused to follow me out the door I always respected his decision. There would always be those who wouldn't believe that, of course, but it was the truth.

The second common accusation was that I was mistreating him by having him on a lead. If I'd had a pound for every time I'd heard someone say 'oh, you shouldn't have him on a leash, he's a cat not a dog' I'd have been a very rich man. I'd explained the reasoning so many times I was bored at hearing myself say the words. On both occasions he'd run off, at Piccadilly Circus and in Islington, he'd been really relieved and clingy when I'd found him. I'd sworn never to let it happen again. But, again, I could keep saying it until I was blue in the face as far as some people were concerned. For them it was an open and shut case: I was some kind of animal abusing monster.

The third, and most upsetting allegation that had been made against me was that I was drugging Bob. I'd only heard that a couple of times, thankfully. But it cut me to the quick both times. Given what I'd been through in the past ten years and the battle I'd fought to kick my heroin habit, I found that the most hurtful insult of all. I found it really, really offensive.

As I watched the Inspector checking Bob I felt pretty certain that someone had raised one, two or even all three of these issues with the RSPCA. But I knew she wasn't going to tell me, not until she'd completed her examination and written some kind of report, at least.

She took out a microchip reading device to check that he was micro-chipped, which he was, of course. The device showed up my name and address as Bob's legal owner.

'That's a good start,' she smiled. 'You'd be surprised how many cat owners don't chip their pets, even these days.'

She then checked his fur for fleas, took a look at his teeth and checked his breath, I assumed to see if there was anything wrong with his liver or maybe his kidneys. She also checked his eyes to see if they were cloudy. That made me wonder whether someone had tried to accuse me of drugging him. It made my blood boil to think someone would say that to the RSPCA.

I didn't bother busking while all this was going on. Instead I reassured the small scrum of people who had stopped that everything was OK. I just hoped it was.

As I paced around I tried to put all those thoughts to the back of my head. I had to be positive, I told myself. I hadn't done anything wrong.

After a few minutes she'd finished the inspection and started asking me questions.

'Any health problems that you are aware of, James?' she asked me, her pen poised over her notebook.

'No,' I said. I made sure to tell her that I regularly took him to the weekly drop-in Blue Cross clinic in Islington. They had always praised me for the way I looked after him and always gave him a clean bill of health. 'They've not spotted anything so I think he's pretty healthy,' I told her.

'That's good to know, James,' she said. 'So tell me, how did you two get together in the first place?'

I told her the story and she nodded and smiled throughout.

'Sounds like you two were meant to be together,' she laughed.

She seemed pretty happy with everything, in fact she looked up and gave me a smile.

'He's a fine fellow, isn't he? Don't suppose you have a phone number that I can reach you on,' she asked.

My battered old Nokia was still working – just – so I gave her the number.

'OK, well I'm happy for now but I may need to follow up with another visit. Are you here every day?'

'Yeah, pretty much most days at the moment,' I said, already feeling uneasy.

'OK, I will give you a call or drop in to see you soon.'

She then gave Bob a final ruffle and headed off into the crowds.

On the one hand I was pleased that she had left without any major drama. All sorts of scenarios had been going through my head. What if she'd found something that I didn't know about, health wise? What if she'd said she needed to take him away? That was the worst conceivable outcome as far as I was concerned. I would have been sick with worry.

But my relief was tempered by other worries.

I knew the RSPCA had significant powers when it came to pet owners, from being able to confiscate a pet, to starting legal proceedings against anyone deemed to be guilty of abusing an animal. Why was she doing a follow-up visit? What was she going to tell her superiors? What sort of report was she going to write? What if I was prosecuted and, heaven forbid, Bob was taken away from me? I couldn't help all these things going through my head, however little control I had over the situation.

I gave myself a good talking to. I was being paranoid again. That wasn't going to happen. There was no reason for it. I had to put those thoughts to one side.

As I headed home that evening, however, I still had a knot of anxiety in my stomach. I had an awful feeling that this was going to hang over me for a while.

It was about a week later when the RSPCA inspector appeared again. She was a lot friendlier and more relaxed this time. Bob responded well to her as well as she once more knelt down to check him out.

I felt a bit more confident this time so engaged her in conversation.

Again, she made some notes and asked me a couple of questions about what we'd been up to that week and what we had planned in the coming days.

She sat and watched us interacting together and with the passers-by. RSPCA inspectors are obviously trained to read animal behaviours and she could see that he was perfectly content to be there and to be doing his little stunts for his audience.

She then headed off again and said she'd be in touch very soon. As she left, she gave Bob another friendly stroke, shook my hand and smiled.

I carried on for an hour or so, but my heart wasn't in it. I was about to pack up when I saw a familiar face striding over. It was the housing manager of one of the blocks of flats on Neal Street. We'd clashed before, over my busking, which she objected to for some reason. She had a face like thunder. She had obviously been watching from a window and had seen the RSPCA officer shaking my hand and walking off.

'People are trying to sleep upstairs,' she said.

'It's two o'clock in the afternoon,' I said, genuinely baffled.

'Never mind that,' she said as if I was some three-year-old child. 'You shouldn't be busking here. Can't you read the sign?', she said, pointing at a plaque across the road on the side of the building where she worked.

'But I'm not busking there, I'm busking on the other side of the road,' I said. 'And I am entitled to do that if I want. The outreach workers and even the Police have told me as much.'

Again, she wasn't interested in having a debate about it. She just wanted to rant and rave at me.

'I've had enough of you and that bloody cat, I'm going to call the police and have you removed,' she said, marching off. She seemed even angrier than when she'd arrived.

Her argument was actually ridiculous. How on earth could I disturb people from their sleep in the middle of the afternoon? I didn't have an amplifier, so it wasn't as if I was blasting out a huge amount of sound. And besides, this was a busy street with a lot of traffic passing through at all hours of the day and night. If anything was going to wake up her residents, it was the constant din of delivery vans and lorries and police sirens. It was crazy.

Despite all this, however, I knew that she did have the law on her side to an extent. There were restrictions on busking in the area and I had to be very careful. So I kept an eagle eye out for the police for the rest of the afternoon.

Sure enough, about half an hour after I'd had the confrontation with the lady, I saw a Police van drawing into the street a hundred yards or so away from our pitch.

'Don't like the look of that, Bob,' I said, unstrapping my guitar and packing up.

By the time two policemen had walked over, I was ready to leave.

'You have to move on,' they said.

'Yes, I know. I'm off,' I said.

The incident had really riled me. I became

convinced that this lady was the one who had reported me to the RSPCA. Now that tactic seemed to have failed, she had changed tack. She would go to any lengths to drive us away, it seemed.

Back at the flat that evening, the RSPCA inspector rang me on my mobile and said that I had absolutely nothing to worry about.

'He's a special creature, and you're doing a grand job,' the lady said. 'My advice to you is to ignore those who tell you any different.' It was the wisest advice I'd had for a long time. And, unusually for me, I took it.

Chapter 16

Doctor Bob

I was finding it harder and harder to haul myself out of bed in the morning. For the past few weeks I'd actually grown to dread the sight of the late winter sun, leaking light through my bedroom window.

It wasn't that I didn't want to get up. I wasn't sleeping well and was usually awake by first light in any case. My reasons for wanting to hide, motionless under the duvet, were very different. I knew that the moment I got up, I would just start coughing again.

I'd suffered from chest problems for some time, but recently they had begun to get really bad. I reasoned it was because I was always on the streets, working outside. But now, no sooner had I got up in the morning, than my lungs and chest were filling up with phlegm and I was coughing really violently almost constantly. At times it was so bad that I was doubling up in pain and I would begin retching and vomiting. It really wasn't pleasant for me – or anyone else, to be honest. The sounds I was making were pretty horrendous. I was embarrassed to be in public places.

I was getting really worried about it. I'd been smoking since I was a 13-year-old back in Australia and had inhaled a lot more than just plain cigarettes over the years. Also, an ex-girlfriend from way back had died of tuberculosis after smoking a lot of drugs a few years earlier. The memory of her coughing uncontrollably in her final months had remained with me. I'd heard somewhere that TB was actually contagious. Had I contracted it from her? Were my lungs collapsing? Try as I might, I couldn't stop all sorts of crazy thoughts whizzing around in my head.

I had tried to get rid of the coughing by dosing myself with cheap medicines from the supermarket. But it had gotten me nowhere. I'd seen a doctor, but at that stage it could easily have been a seasonal cold and he'd fobbed me off with a suggestion that I should take a few paracetamol, rest and cut down on smoking. That hadn't achieved much at all.

Bob had again sensed I was unwell and started paying me attention. He would wrap himself around me as if taking some kind of measurements. I'd learned the lessons of the past and didn't dismiss him this time.

'Here comes Doctor Bob,' I joked one day.

There was no question in my mind that he was performing some kind of diagnosis. When I was lying on the sofa or on the bed, he would often spread himself out on my chest, purring gently.

I'd read about cats having the power to heal bones with their purring. Apparently there's something about the frequency at which they vibrate that somehow strengthens bones. I wondered whether he was trying to somehow heal my chest. More worryingly, I wondered whether he knew something I didn't?

In a way, that was the scariest thing of all. I knew how intuitive cats are when it comes to sniffing out illness in humans. There's evidence that they can predict epileptic fits, seizures and other illnesses. One cat I read about, from Yorkshire, would give its male owner 'strange looks' before he was about to have a fit. Famously, there was a cat called Oscar who lived in an old people's home in America and would come and sit with residents who were in their final hours. No one was quite sure whether he was picking up on something visual or whether he was able to tune into the smells produced by the bio-chemical changes in a person's body when they die. What was in no doubt, however, was the fact that Oscar's ability to anticipate people's passing was uncanny, so much so that people dreaded seeing him sidling up to them. It was as if the cat

was some kind of Angel of Death. I did hope Bob
wasn't the same.

After a while I made another appointment, this
time with a young doctor that a friend had recommended as being very good. He certainly seemed a
little more sympathetic. I told him about the coughing and the vomiting.

'I'd better take a listen to your lungs,' he said.
After checking me out with a stethoscope he made
me do a peak-flow check, testing the strength of
my breathing and chest. I'd had childhood asthma
so I knew my chest wasn't the strongest.

He didn't say too much. He just sat there making
notes, rather too many of them for my liking.

'OK, Mr Bowen, I'd like you to have a chest
X-ray,' he said, eventually.

'Oh, OK,' I said, worried already.

He then printed out a form which he handed to
me.

'Take this along to Homerton Hospital and
they'll know what to do,' he said.

I knew he was being careful in his language. But
there was something about his face that spooked
me a little. I didn't like it.

I took the form home and stuck it on the

sideboard in the front room. I then quietly forgot about it. A small part of me couldn't face the hassle. It wasn't that long ago that I'd been hospitalised with DVT. What if I had to be admitted again? What if it was something even worse? I really didn't like hospitals.

On top of this, I'd been to Homerton Hospital before and I knew it was a nightmare. I pictured in my mind one of those long days waiting in a queue and just getting frustrated. I told myself that I couldn't afford to waste a day there not earning money.

Of course, these were all rather limp excuses. The truth was that I was terrified of what an X-ray might find. It was pure, ostrich-like stubbornness. I assumed that if I stuck my head in the sand and forgot all about it, the coughing and vomiting and all the other unpleasantness would simply go away. Of course it didn't. It only got worse.

I reached breaking point one day when I visited the publishers. I had, at last, begun to believe that the book was finally happening. They'd mocked up a cover, with Bob sitting Zen-like on my rucksack. On the back was a picture of me, while inside was a brief note on 'the author'. I still had to pinch myself to believe it was happening. Unfortunately, I'd had a coughing fit in the middle of the meeting. I'd began retching and could feel like I was ready to throw up. So I'd made an excuse about needing the toilet and dashed off there. I'm sure they had their suspicions that I was up to no good and I wouldn't have blamed them if they did. I was a recovering drug addict, after all.

I knew it must have looked pretty bad, and that I couldn't repeat it in March. The publication of the book was looming into view and I'd been told that I might be doing a few media interviews, even an appearance on television. There was also talk of book signings where I'd meet members of the public. It all seemed pretty far-fetched, but to be on the safe side I decided I had to get to the bottom of this and go for the X-ray.

By now I'd lost the form, so I went back to the surgery to see the same doctor.

'You don't seem to have had your X-ray,' he said, scrolling through the records on his computer.

'No, erm, I didn't go. I haven't had time. I'd lose a day if I went there,' I said, slightly embarrassed. 'I've been writing a book.'

'OK,' he said, looking at me disbelievingly then tapping away and then printing out another form.

'This is for an emergency appointment. It's a walk-in service. You won't have to hang around for long.'

'OK,' I said, a little reluctantly.

I knew that, this time, I couldn't really duck out of it.

I went along to Homerton and was led into a

large room by a couple of nurses, one of whom asked me to take off my shirt and stand in a contraption. She then proceeded to place a big metal plate on my chest before retiring behind a screen.

Again, it could have been paranoia on my part but I was disconcerted by the fact that she wrote a lot of notes afterwards.

'How did it look?' I asked her, fishing for a clue.

'Fine, but we will send a full report to your doctor. Should be there in a few days.'

I took some solace from her reassurance, but was still a bundle of nerves for the next 72 hours.

I went along to see the doctor with a real sense of foreboding.

I have a tendency to think the worst so I was braced to hear something terrible. I was slightly taken aback when the doctor looked at the notes attached to his copy of the X-ray images and said: 'Your lungs are completely clear, Mr Bowen.'

'Really?' I said.

'Yes. There's not a single black spot, which is frankly remarkable given that you tell me you've been smoking since you were 13.'

'In fact,' he continued, 'I would go so far as to say that you seem to have super healthy lungs,' he added.

'So why am I coughing my guts up all the time?' I asked, confused.

'I suspect you've got an infection of some kind.

Nothing has shown up in the tests we've done. But I think your lungs are simply trying to expel all the rubbish that they are accumulating there. So let's try and treat the infection,' he said, prescribing me some heavy duty antibiotics.

'That's it? Antibiotics,' I said, relieved but slightly shocked to discover it was that simple.

'Well, let's see if they work,' he said. 'If not we will have to explore things a bit more.'

I was sceptical. It couldn't be that simple, I told myself. But it was. Within days my chest was feeling much better and the coughing was easing off.

My agent, Mary, had been worried about my health. She'd been anxious that the publicity and the signings that would soon be coming up might be too much for me. She had my best interests at heart, I knew that.

'You seem a lot better,' she told me when we met for a chat about the publication of the book which was now just weeks away.

But it was when I got another opinion that I really knew I was in the clear.

I was lying on the bed reading a comic book. Out of nowhere, Bob appeared and jumped up. He slid up to me in the same way he had done over the previous few weeks, placing himself on my chest and purring quietly away. After a moment or two, he put his ear to my chest, doing his feline stethoscope act. He lay there for a moment, listening intently. And then, as quickly as he'd arrived, he'd gone. He just picked himself up and hopped off the bed in the direction of his favourite radiator. I couldn't help smiling.

'Thanks, Doctor Bob,' I said.

Chapter 17

Basic Instincts

They say that March comes in like a lion and goes out like a lamb. The month had barely begun but the weather was already living up to its reputation. There were days when the wind blowing down the alleyways of Soho and the West End made such a raw, rasping noise it could almost have been a lion's roar. Some days I struggled to feel the tips of my fingers as I played my guitar. Fortunately, Bob was a little better insulated than me.

Even now with spring around the corner, he was still sporting his rather luxurious winter coat. His midriff was also still carrying some of the extra weight he'd put on over Christmas. The cold hardly seemed to bother him at all.

Bob and I missed Angel, but if I was honest, we were enjoying life more in Covent Garden.

We'd become a double act and seemed somehow more at home amongst the jugglers and fire-eaters, human statues and other street performers that roamed the Piazza and surrounding streets. It was a competitive place, of course, so, as we settled back into daily life in central London, we polished up our act.

Sometimes I would play my guitar while sitting cross-legged on the pavement with him. He'd always loved that and would drape himself across the body of my guitar, just like he'd done during our early days together, years earlier. We shook hands and he'd stand on his hind legs to collect treats. We also had a new party piece.

It had been born back at the flat one day while he had been playing with Belle. As usual, he was tossing his shabby old scraggedy mouse around. Belle wanted to take it off him so that she could give it a decent wash.

'God knows what germs it's collecting, Bob,' I heard her telling him. 'It needs a good scrubbing.'

He was reluctant to surrender his precious plaything. He always was. So she offered him a treat. Choosing between the two was a real dilemma and he dithered for a second before going for the treat. He released the mouse from his jaws long enough to receive the little snack – and for Belle to whisk the toy from under his nose.

'Well done, Bob,' she said afterwards.

'Give me five,' she said, putting her hand in the air like an American footballer or basketball player, inviting his team-mates to celebrate a score.

I was sitting there and saw him raise his paw to give her an acknowledegment. 'That was cool,' I laughed. 'Bet you can't get him to do it again.'

'Bet I can,' Belle said, before proceeding to do exactly that.

Since then he'd come to associate it with receiving a treat. On Neal Street it had pulled in all sorts of admirers, including some rather famous ones.

It was around 4pm on a Saturday afternoon and a couple of little girls had stopped to admire Bob. They were about nine or ten years old and were accompanied by a small group of adults, including a couple of big, burly bouncer-like guys in dark glasses. To judge by the way they were anxiously surveying the scene while the girls stroked Bob they must have been security minders.

'Daddy, look at this,' one of the girls said excitedly.

'Oh yeah. That's a cool cat,' a voice said.

I froze to the spot. I recognised the voice immediately.

'It can't be,' I said. But it was.

I turned round and standing behind me was the unmistakeable figure of Sir Paul McCartney.

I wouldn't have expected one of the greatest figures in popular music of all time to engage with a lowly street performer. He was, after all, in a slightly different league to me when it came to knocking out a tune. But he seemed charming.

I had my early edition of the book alongside me on the floor and saw it catch his eye. I also had a wad of flyers advertising the first book signing the publishers had organised. It was now just three days away.

The event was going to mark the beginning – and probably the end – of my career as a published author. I was feeling apprehensive about it already and had been frantically handing the flyers out to anyone who showed an interest, in the hope that I'd at least avoid the embarrassment of sitting in an empty bookshop the following week. I felt sure if I fished around in the bins of Covent Garden I'd find most of them there.

Inside my head a little voice was saying *oh, go on, give him one*.

'Erm, I've written a book about me and Bob,' motioning to my ginger companion sitting at my feet. 'I'm having a signing next week if you want to come along,' I said, handing him the flyer.

To my amazement he took it.

'I'll take a look,' he said.

By now a sizable crowd had begun to form around us and his minders were getting a bit twitchy. People were flashing away with their cameras. For once it wasn't Bob they were snapping.

'We'd better move along kids,' the lady with him said. By now I'd worked out who she was. It was Sir Paul's new wife, Nancy Shevell, who he'd married the previous autumn. She seemed really cool.

'Take care man and keep it going,' Sir Paul said as he hooked his arm into hers and rushed off with his entourage.

I was slightly dizzy afterwards. Starstruck I suppose would have been a more accurate description. I stayed in Neal Street for another hour or so but headed home on Cloud Nine.

There wasn't a snowball's chance in hell of Sir Paul McCartney coming along to the signing. Why would he come? No one else was going to show up, I said to myself. All that really didn't matter now. If it achieved nothing else and sold only five copies, the book had already allowed me to achieve the impossible. I'd chatted to a member of The Beatles.

Bob attracted so much attention these days that small crowds would often gather around us. Late on the afternoon of the Monday after I'd met the McCartneys, a dozen or so Spanish-speaking students were clustered on the pavement, each of them snapping away with their cameras and phones. It was always great to meet people, it was part of the attraction of what I did. But it could be distracting and, given the nature of street life, getting distracted was never a great idea.

As the crowd broke up and headed off in the direction of Covent Garden, I sat down on the pavement to give Bob a couple of treats. With the light already beginning to fade, the chill was really setting in again. Tomorrow was the day of the book signing in Islington. I wanted to get a reasonably early night, although I knew I wouldn't sleep much. I also didn't want to keep Bob out for much longer. As I stroked him, I noticed immediately that his body language was very defensive. His back was arched and his body was stiff. He wasn't much interested in the food either which was always a sign something was wrong. Instead, his eyes were fixed on something in the near distance. Something – or someone – was clearly bothering him.

I looked across the street and saw a rough-looking character who was sitting, staring at us.

Living your life on the streets, you develop an instant radar when it comes to people. I could spot a bad apple instantly. This guy looked rotten to the core. He was a little bit older than me, in his late thirties probably. He was wearing battered jeans and had a denim jacket. He was sitting on the pavement, legs crossed, rolling up a cigarette and sipping on a can of cheap lager. It was obvious what he was looking at – and what his intentions were. He was working out how to relieve me of my money.

In the space of the last few minutes, most of the Spanish students and several others had dropped coins into my guitar case. One rather cool-looking black guy had given me £5. We'd probably collected £20 in the space of half an hour. I knew better than to leave too much money on display to the world and had scooped up most of it, slipping it in my rucksack. He'd obviously registered this.

I wasn't going to confront him, however. As long as he kept his distance, there was no need. I'd been in his shoes myself. I knew how desperate people could get. I sensed he was trouble, but unless he proved that I was going to give him the benefit of the doubt. Let him cast the first stone and all that, I said to myself.

Just to make sure, however, I looked across at him and nodded, as if to say: 'I've spotted you, and I know what you're thinking. So just forget about it.'

Street people speak the same language. We can convey a hundred words with a simple look or expression, so he understood me immediately. He just growled, got himself up and slinked off. He knew he'd been rumbled and didn't like it. He was soon heading off in the direction of Shaftesbury Avenue, probably to prey on someone else.

The instant the guy disappeared around the corner, Bob's body language lightened and he had a renewed interest in the snacks.

'Don't worry, mate,' I said, slipping a little biscuit into his mouth. 'He's gone on his way. We won't see him again.'

The street was particularly busy that day and we'd soon collected more than enough to get Bob and me a few days' worth of shopping in our local shop. When I started packing up, Bob didn't need a second invitation to jump up on to my shoulders. It was getting colder by the minute.

I knew he'd need to do his business before we got the bus home, so we headed for his regular spot outside the posh office block on Endell Street.

To get to this spot we had to walk down one of the narrower and less well lit streets in the area. As we did so, the world suddenly turned quiet. London could be like that at times. One minute it was full to bursting, the next it was deserted. It was part of the city's many contradictions.

I was halfway down the street when I felt Bob moving on my shoulder. At first I thought he was simply dying to go to the toilet.

'Hold on for another second, mate,' I said. 'We're almost there.'

But I soon realised he was repositioning himself and, unusually for him, had turned himself to look backwards rather than forwards.

'What's wrong, Bob?' I said, turning around.

I looked down the street. There was a guy locking up his coffee shop for the evening and that was about it. I thought nothing more of it. The coast seemed clear enough to me.

Bob didn't seem quite so convinced. Something was definitely bothering him.

I'd barely taken a dozen steps when all of a sudden he made the loudest noise I'd ever heard him make. It was like a primal scream, a piercing *wheeeeeow* followed by a really loud hissed *hsssssssss*. At the same time I felt a tug on my rucksack and then an almighty scream, this time from a human.

I swung round to see the bloke who had been staring at us earlier on Neal Street. He was bent over double and was holding his hand. I could see the back of it and saw that there were huge scratches. Blood was gushing from his wounds.

It was obvious what had happened. He had made a lunge for my rucksack. Bob must have dropped himself over my back and lashed out with his claws. He'd dug them deep into this guy's hands, ripping into the skin. He was still in fighting mood too.

Bob was standing on my shoulder, snarling and hissing.

But the guy wasn't finished. He lunged at me with his fists but I managed to dodge him. It was hard to do much with Bob balanced on my shoulder, but I landed a well-directed kick to the guy's leg. I was wearing my really heavy Dr. Martens boots so it had the desired effect and he dropped to his knees for a second.

He was soon back on his feet, though. For a moment we just stood there shouting at each other.

'F***ing cat, look what it's done to my f***ing hand,' he said, waving his bleeding arm at me in the gloom.

'Serves you right, you were going to mug me,' I said.

'I'll f***ing kill it if I see it again,' he said pointing at Bob. There was another brief standoff while the guy looked around the street. He found a small piece of wood which he waved at me a couple of times. Bob was screeching and hissing at him more animatedly than ever. The guy took one step towards us with the piece of wood then thought better of it and just tossed it to one side. After letting fly with another stream of expletives, he turned on his heels and stumbled off into the gloom, still holding his hand.

On the bus back home, Bob sat on my lap. He was purring steadily and had tucked his head under

my arm, as he often did when he – or I – felt vulnerable. I guessed we were both feeling that way after
our encounter, but I couldn't be sure, of course.

That was the joy and frustration of having a cat.
'Cats are mysterious kind of folk – there is more
passing in their minds than we are aware of,' Sir
Walter Scott wrote. Bob was more mysterious than
most. In many ways, that was part of his magic,
what made him such an extraordinary companion.
We had been through so much together, yet he still
had the ability to startle and surprise me. He'd
done it again this evening.

We'd had our fair share of confrontations over
the years, but we'd never been attacked like this.
And I'd never seen him react and defend me in that
way either. I'd not been switched on to the threat
this guy posed at all, but Bob had.

How had he sensed the guy was not to be trusted
from the minute he set eyes on him? I could read
the signs from a human perspective, but how did
he know that? And how had he detected his presence when we were walking away from Neal
Street? I'd seen no sign of him anywhere. Had Bob
caught a glimpse of him hiding in an alleyway?
Had he smelled him?

I didn't know. I just had to accept that Bob
possessed abilities and instincts that were beyond
my understanding – and would probably always
remain that way.

That was the frustrating part. He was exhilarating company at times, but he was also an enigma. I would never truly know what went on in his feline brain. Yes, we were best friends. We had an almost telepathic bond. Instinctively, we knew what each other were thinking at times. But that understanding didn't extend to being able to share our deepest thoughts. We couldn't really tell each other what we felt. As silly as it sounded, I often felt sad about that. And I did so now.

Holding him close to me as the bus lurched its way through the London traffic, I had an almost overwhelming urge to know what emotions he'd gone through back there in the side street. Had he been scared? Or had he just fallen back on his basic instincts? Had he just sensed the need to defend himself – and me – and acted? Had he just dealt with it in the moment? And did that mean that he'd already forgotten about it? Or was he thinking the same kind of thoughts as me? I am fed up with this life. *I am sick of having to look over my shoulder all the time. I want to live in a safer, gentler, happier world.*

I suspected I knew the answer. Of course he'd rather not be fighting off scumbags on the streets. Of course, he'd rather be sitting somewhere warm rather than freezing on a pavement. What creature wouldn't?

As my mind ticked over, I dipped into my pocket

and pulled out a scrunched up flyer. It was one of the last that I had. I'd given the rest away. It had a photo of me with Bob on my shoulders and read:

Come and meet
James Bowen and Bob the cat
James and Bob will be signing copies of
their new book
A STREET CAT NAMED BOB
at Waterstones, Islington Green, London
on Tuesday 13th March 2012 at 6pm

Bob looked at it and tilted his head ever-so-slightly. It was, again, as if he recognised the image of the pair of us.

I stared at the scrap of paper for what must have been a couple of minutes, lost in my thoughts.

I'd been wrestling with the same old questions for so long now. Truth be told, I was thoroughly sick of them. But tonight had brought them to the fore again. How many more times would I have to put myself and Bob in the firing line? Would I ever break this cycle and get us off the streets?

I flattened the flyer out neatly and folded it away in my pocket.

'I hope this is the answer, Bob,' I said. 'I really do.'

Chapter 18

Waiting for Bob

It was barely 9am but my stomach was already churning away like a cement mixer.

I'd made some toast but couldn't touch it for fear of being physically sick. If I felt like this now, I asked myself, how on earth was I going to feel in nine hours' time?

The publishers had organised the signing, thinking it would be a good opportunity to generate some London publicity, and maybe attract a few people to buy a copy or two at the same time. As well as handing out flyers down in Covent Garden I had even detoured via Angel a couple of times. We still had a few friends there, thankfully.

Waterstones in Islington had been the obvious venue. The store was part of my story in more ways than one. Not only had the staff there helped us when we'd had nowhere to go a year or so earlier, they even featured in one of the more dramatic scenes in the book. One weekday evening, I'd run in the front door, desperate and panic-stricken, when Bob had run off after being scared by an aggressive dog at Angel tube station.

In the days running up to the event I'd started giving interviews to more newspapers but also to radio and television. To help me get used to this, I'd been sent to a specialist media trainer in central London. It was a bit intimidating. I had to sit in a sound-proofed room having myself recorded and then analysed by an expert. But he had been gentle with me and had taught me a few tricks of the trade. During one of the first recordings, for instance, I'd made the classic mistake of fiddling with a pen while talking. When it was played back to me all I could hear was the sound of me tapping the pen against the desk like some manic rock drummer. It was incredibly distracting and annoying.

The trainer prepared me for the sort of questions I could expect. He predicted, quite rightly, that most people would want to know how I'd ended up on the streets, how Bob had helped changed my life and what the future held for us both. He also prepared me to answer questions about whether I was clean of drugs, which I was happy to do. I felt I had nothing to hide.

The pieces the newspapers and bloggers had been writing were almost universally nice. A writer from the *London Evening Standard* had said some lovely things about Bob, writing that he 'has entranced London like no feline since the days of Dick Whittington'. But he also upset me a little by writing about the holes in my jeans and my 'blackened teeth and nails'. He also described me as having the 'pleading manner of someone who is used to being ignored'. I'd been warned to expect that kind of thing; it went with the territory and the bottom line was that I knew I was 'damaged goods' as that same writer called me. It wasn't pleasant though.

The signing had been scheduled two days ahead of the official publication date, March 15th, which also happened to be my 33rd birthday.

I hoped that wasn't going to put a hex on everything. Birthdays hadn't exactly been a cause for celebration in my life, certainly not since my teens.

I had spent my 13th birthday in a children's ward at the Princess Margaret Children's Hospital in Western Australia. It had been a miserable time in my young life and had only accelerated my downward spiral. Not long afterwards I'd started sniffing glue and experimenting with marijuana. It was the start of my long descent into drug addiction.

Fast forward ten years, to my 23rd birthday, and

I'd been on the streets of London. I might have spent it in a hostel, but I could just as easily have been sleeping rough in an alleyway around Charing Cross. At that point my life was at rock bottom and I had absolutely no recollection of it. The days, weeks, months and years had all blended into each other. The chances are that, if I had been aware it was my birthday, I'd have spent the day trying to beg, borrow or – most likely – steal the money I needed to treat myself to an extra wrap of heroin. I'd probably taken the same reckless gamble I'd taken a hundred times before and risked overdosing by taking an 'extra hit'. I could easily have ended up like that guy I'd seen on the landing of my flats.

Ten years further down the road, my life had finally taken a positive turn. That period now seemed like another life and another world. When I looked back I found it hard to believe that I'd lived through that period. But, for good or bad, it would always be a part of me. It was certainly a part of the book. I'd decided not to sugar-coat my story. It was virtually all there, warts and all, which was another one of the reasons I felt so racked with nerves.

In the hours before the signing, I was due to be filmed by a photographer and cameraman from the Reuters international news agency. He wanted to take a series of photos of Bob and I going about our normal, day-to-day life, travelling around on the tube then busking on Neal Street. I was quite glad of the distraction. By the time I'd finished with the photographer, it was early evening.

A damp chill was beginning to descend when we got back to Islington and made the familiar walk from Angel tube station. There was no sign of the guy who had 'acquired' my pitch outside the tube station. A flower seller told me that the guy and his dog had been causing all sorts of trouble and had already been stripped of the pitch by the co-ordinators. There was now no one from *The Big Issue* selling magazines outside Angel.

'What a waste,' I said. 'I'd built that pitch up into a nice earner for someone.' But that wasn't my concern any more. I had other things to worry about.

Bob and I walked through Islington Memorial Park towards Waterstones. We were early so I let Bob do his business and sat on the bench to enjoy a quiet cigarette. Part of me felt like a condemned man, enjoying a final, fleeting moment of pleasure before going to face the firing squad. But another part of me felt a sense of anticipation. I felt like I was on the verge of a fresh start in my life; that, for want of a better phrase, a new chapter in my life was beginning.

I felt queasier than ever. I had so many conflicting thoughts fighting for space in my head. What if no one turned up? What if loads of people turned up and thought the book was rubbish? How would Bob react if there was a crowd? How would people react to me? I wasn't a typical author. I wasn't a polished public personality. I was a guy who was still operating on the fringes of society. Or at least, that's how it felt. I knew people would love Bob, but I was terrified that they'd hate me.

I drew on the last remnant of my cigarette, making it last for as long as possible. The nerves had solidified inside me to such an extent that I felt like someone had punched me really hard in the stomach.

Luckily Bob was being extra cool for both of us. He spent a couple of minutes rooting around in a favourite little spot then sauntered back to me. He just gave me a look as if to say: 'it's all right, mate, it's all good.'

It was uncanny how he was able to calm me.

Arriving at the bookshop about half an hour before the signing was due to start, there were four or five people standing in line outside. *Ah well, someone has turned up at least*, I said to myself, relieved. They all smiled at us and I gave them a sheepish wave. I couldn't quite get my head round the idea that people were giving up an hour of their evening to come and meet us. There were a few more people inside the store as well. They were all stood in a queue to pay and were all holding copies of the book.

Alan, the manager, invited me upstairs to the staff room where I could wait for the signing to start.

'You can have a glass of wine and Bob can have a saucer of milk. You can take it easy for a minute before things get under way,' he said, sensing my nervousness.

I wasn't sure whether to keep a clear head or to have a drink for Dutch courage. I decided on the former. I'd have a glass of wine afterwards.

Belle, Mary, Garry and a bunch of people from the publishers were there to wish me luck. There was also a stack of books for me to sign for general sale in the store. Someone had come up with the rather bright idea of having a paw-shaped stamp so that Bob could also 'sign' each book. I got to work scrawling on the first copies. Belle added the final flourishing touch with the paw stamps. There were at least two dozen books in the pile. Were they sure they'd even sell this many?

The staff from the store seemed positive. At one point one of them arrived beaming.

'It's stretching all the way around the block,' she smiled.

'What is?' I said, stupidly.

'The queue. It's stretching all the way back around the corner. There's probably a hundred people there with more joining all the time.'

I was speechless. I didn't think it was possible to feel any more anxious, but somehow I did. There was an open window next to me. For a moment, I thought about climbing out of it, shinning my way down the drainpipes and making a hasty escape.

As the clock ticked down towards 6pm, Bob climbed up on my shoulder and we headed back down to the main store. On the landing at the bottom of the first flight of stairs, I knelt down and took a sneaky look down on to the shop floor. My heart jumped into my throat. It was heaving with people.

A table stacked with books had been laid out ready for me and Bob. The line of people waiting to file past it was stretching along the bookshelves all the way to the entrance and out into the dark March evening. They were right. There must have been a hundred people and more in it. At the other side of the store, a separate queue of people were lined up, buying copies of the book. There was even a group of photographers and a television cameraman there.

It was surreal, an out-of-body experience. Until now we'd been hidden from view but as we started walking down the final flight of steps, the cameras began flashing and photographers began shouting.

'Bob, Bob, this way, Bob.'

There was even a ripple of applause and a couple of cheers.

My years on the street with Bob had taught me to expect the unexpected. We'd learned to adapt, to roll with the punches, sometimes literally. This time, however, it felt like we were entering totally uncharted territory.

One thing was clear, however. We'd come too far to pass on this chance. If we took it, our time on the street might, just might, start drawing to a close. That new chapter might just open up for us.

'Come on, Bob,' I whispered, stroking the back of his neck before taking a final, deep breath. 'No turning back now.'

Epilogue

Always

That night in March 2012 was probably the most important of my life. Afterwards there were no more doubts. It really was a new beginning for me and Bob. The book signing in Islington was a success way beyond my expectations. Paul McCartney didn't quite make it, but more than 300 other people did. The numbers clamouring to meet us caught everyone by surprise, even the book-shop, who were cleaned out of every one of their 200 or so copies within half an hour.

'So much for my prediction that we'd only sell half a dozen,' I joked with Alan, the store manager, when I eventually got to share a glass of wine with him after three hours of signing and interviews.

No one could work out how we'd drawn such a big crowd. The flyers and the publicity had obvi-ously played their part. We'd set up a Twitter account which had attracted a hundred or so followers, but even then it didn't quite explain the passion with which people had embraced Bob and myself.

It was the first sign that something amazing was about to take place.

When *A Street Cat Named Bob* went on general sale two days later it seemed to strike an immediate chord and became, what *The Times* described as, 'an instantly bestselling memoir'. It entered the bestseller list on the first weekend after publication – and remained in the UK bestseller list for the best part of a year, most of that time at No 1. Each Sunday, I would pick up a newspaper and look at the latest chart, shaking my head slowly. Why was it so popular? What had captured the public's imagination? After a while I gave up trying to work it out. Even more miraculously, the book swiftly found a foreign audience too. At the last count, it was set to be translated into 26 other languages. In Italy it was *A Spasso Con Bob (A Walk with Bob)*. In Portugal it was *Minha História Con Bob (My Story with Bob)*. It seemed to have some universal appeal. Whatever the language, people seemed to love the story, and most of all, of course, they simply adored Bob.

As a result, Bob and I became, to all intents and purposes, minor celebrities, appearing on television and radio programmes to talk about the book and its popularity. It wasn't something for which I was prepared, even after my afternoon of media training. Our first major appearance, on the BBC's

Breakfast programme was typical. I arrived at the studios in West London at the crack of dawn a bundle of nerves. I was paranoid that Bob would be scared of the lights or the strange surroundings. But he'd taken to it all, sitting on the sofa serenely watching himself on the monitors in front of him. He'd naturally been the star of the show, even managing to do a series of high fives for the hosts who seemed to be every bit as bewitched by him as everyone else. It was the same when I made other appearances.

Wherever we went I was asked the same questions. In particular, people would begin to wonder how the success of the book was changing life for the both of us.

The most significant and obvious change was that Bob and I no longer needed to put ourselves in harm's way on the streets. It took a little while for the financial rewards of the book's success to trickle in, so for a few months we had continued to busk on Neal Street. Gradually, however, we were able to ration our appearances. It was such a huge relief to wake up each morning knowing we wouldn't have to face the cold and the rain and that I wouldn't have to experience that sense of uncertainty and quiet desperation that I felt each day I used to set off for Angel or Covent Garden.

A small part of us would always remain there of course. You can take the busker off the street . . . and Bob has always loved the attention he gets from admirers. So we continued to make occasional appearances, the only difference being that we now did so in order to help other people rather than ourselves.

At the beginning of 2013, for instance, we formed a relationship with the animal charity, Blue Cross. We began collecting money for them both online and via public appearances and our occasional days busking. We raised almost £5,000 in the first week. It felt fantastic to be able to give something back. They were so kind to me during my early days with Bob and continued to help us when we popped into their weekly clinics on Islington Green. I remembered how I'd often felt that Bob was my reward for some act of kindness that I'd bestowed on someone earlier in my life. I'd felt like it was karma. By adopting the Blue Cross, I felt like I was now reciprocating their generosity, performing another act of karma. I aim to do the same thing for homeless charities at some point in the future.

Of course people also asked me if the book had made me rich. The answer to that was yes and no. Compared to where I'd been financially, I was, by any stretch of the imagination, comfortable. But I didn't become an overnight millionaire. The important thing was that, for the foreseeable future, at least, I knew I wasn't going to be reduced to scouring the shelves of supermarkets for 10p tins of past-the-sell-by-date baked beans. For years I had to rely on my wits and a few state hand-outs. Now, for the first time in many years, I had a bank account and even an accountant to help me manage my affairs, including my taxes. I hadn't earned enough money to be eligible to pay tax in the past decade. The fact that I now began doing so was important to me.

When you are homeless or selling *The Big Issue* you know you aren't contributing to society – and you know that society resents you for that. A lot of people take great pleasure in telling you so. To your face. 'Get a job, you scrounging git,' had been a common refrain for me for a decade. The result of this is that you become gradually more marginalised by that society. People don't understand that the lack of self-esteem and general hopelessness you feel when you are homeless, busking or even selling *The Big Issue* is partly down to this. You want to be part of society, but that society is, effectively, driving you away. It becomes a vicious circle.

Paying my way was the most tangible sign that I was once more 'a member' of society. And it felt good.

There were so many other positives to the book's success.

It improved my relationship with my parents. Among the throng at Waterstones on that March evening was my father, who I'd persuaded to come partly out of curiosity and partly for moral support.

The bewildered but delighted look on his face when he witnessed the queues will live in my memory for a very, very long time. After all the disappointments, I felt like I'd given him something to be proud about. At last.

He was touched when he was shown the note I'd written thanking him and my mum in the acknowledgements. Apparently he shed a tear when he read the book back at home. He called me up to say well done, and said the same thing again on other occasions. He still told me to get a haircut and a shave, of course, but at least he stopped nagging me to 'get a proper job'.

We didn't talk about our feelings about the past in huge detail. That was not his style. He's not the kind of person to have a big heart to heart. I suspect I knew what he was thinking but I also knew that he couldn't express it. He couldn't formulate the words, but that was fine. Knowing was enough for me.

I also travelled to Australia again to spend time with my mother. She'd read the book and wept as well. She told me she felt guilty about many of the things that had happened but was honest enough to say that, as a teenager, I was a nightmare who would have challenged even the most sainted mother. I accepted that.

We were open and honest with each other and realised that we'd be friends from now onwards.

Another satisfying aspect of the book's success was the impact it seemed to have on people's attitude to *The Big Issue* sellers and the homeless in general. Schools and charities wrote, telling me how the story of Bob and I had helped them to better understand the plight of the homeless.

Bob and I were on Facebook and Twitter. Every day it seemed we got a message from someone explaining how they no longer walked past *The Big Issue* vendors. Many told me they now made a point of always engaging them in conversation. I knew I'd had my difficulties with the magazine, but I felt a huge sense of pride in that. It is a fine institution that deserves everyone's support, especially in these dark economic times.

On a more profound level, our story also seemed to connect with people who were facing difficult times in their lives. Hundreds of them wrote to me or contacted us via social media. Some read our story of survival and drew their own strength from it. Others recognised the power animals possess to heal us humans. Again, I was immensely proud every time I received a message of this kind. I never in a million years expected that I'd touch the life of one person, let alone thousands.

A few people got a little carried away and bestowed some kind of divinity on Bob and me. Bob might have been a saint but I wasn't, that was for sure. You can't spend a decade fighting for your day-to-day existence on the streets of London without being shaped by that environment. You can't live a chunk of your life dependent on heroin without being damaged by that experience. I was a product of my past.

So I knew it would take me a long time to iron out the rougher edges of my personality. And I would never quite shake off my past, not least because people would always pop up to remind me of my lost years. Medically, I still carried the scars of my drug-addicted twenties too. The punishment I inflicted on my body would continue to extract a price. In short, Saint James of Tottenham didn't exist. He never had and he never would. The person who most definitely did exist, however, was someone who had been given his second chance in life and who was determined to seize it. And if I ever lost sight of that, I now had constant reminders of why that second chance was so important.

I recently received a letter from a lady in a small, rural community in Wales whose close friend had just lost her long fight against cancer. The lady had given our book to her friend during her final days. She had been so touched by it that she had, in turn, given a copy to her local Minister. During his oration at the friend's funeral in the small village chapel, the Minister had held up a copy of our book in front of the congregation. He mentioned how much the book had meant to the lady at the end of her life and praised our 'wonderful journey of hope'. Bob and I were, he said, an example of the power of 'faith, hope and love'. Reading this moved me to floods of tears. It was unbelievably humbling. It remained in my head for days.

For far too many years those three precious qualities – faith, hope and love – had been sorely missing in my life. But then a twist of fate delivered me all three. They were each embodied in the mischievous, playful, canny, occasionally cantankerous but always devoted cat who helped me turn my life around.

Bob had helped me restore my faith in myself and the world around me. He had shown me hope when I really couldn't see much of it. Most of all he had given me the unconditional love each of us needs.

During one of my television appearances on the BBC, a presenter asked me a question which threw me at first.

'What will you do when Bob is not around any more?' he asked.

I got a little emotional at the very thought of losing him, but once I'd gathered myself, I answered as honestly as I could. I said I knew that animals didn't live as long as us humans, but that I would cherish every single day that I shared with him. And when the time came for him to leave, he would live on in the books that he inspired.

They may have been the truest words I ever uttered.

The world as it was before I met Bob seemed a harsh, heartless and, yes, a hopeless place. The world I have grown to see through his eyes is a very different one. There was a time when I couldn't distinguish one day from the next. Now I cherish each one. I am happier, healthier and more fulfilled than I have ever been. For now, at least, I have escaped from life on the streets. I can see a clear path ahead of me.

I have no idea where our adventure will lead us next. But I know that, for as long as he is around, Bob will be at the heart of all the good things that come to pass. He is my companion, my best friend, my teacher and my soul mate. And he will remain all of those things. Always.

Acknowledgements

Writing this book has been a collaborative process and I need to thank the team of incredibly talented and supportive people who helped me cross the finishing line. Garry Jenkins was my principle guiding hand, skilfully extracting the stories then shaping the manuscript. At Hodder, I have to thank Rowena Webb and Maddy Price along with Ciara Foley, who edited the script. I would also like to single out the brilliant publicists Emma Knight, Kerry Hood and Emilie Ferguson. A big thanks also to Dan Williams for his superb line drawings. At Aitken Alexander I'm totally indebted to my fantastic agent Mary Pachnos as well as the team of Sally Riley, Nishta Hurry, Liv Stones and Matilda Forbes-Watson. Thanks also to Joaquim Fernandes at Aitken Alexander and Raymond Walters at R Walters & Co for their invaluable guidance and help. Closer to home I'd like to thank my best friends Kitty and Ron, for being at my side through what has been a pretty crazy year or so. It hasn't been easy at times, but they've remained steadfast and loyal and I owe them more than I can say. I'd also like to thank my mother and father for their love and support, not just in the past year but throughout the darker and more difficult earlier years when I was, I know, far from the easiest of sons. I can't let this opportunity pass without thanking the legions of people who have written to me either directly or through social media, passing on their good wishes and sharing their experiences. I've done my best to reply to as many as possible but hope that I can be forgiven for not getting back to each and every one of you. The response has been, at times, overwhelming. Most of all, of course, I'd like to thank the little guy who remains my constant companion. I still don't know whether I found Bob or he found me. What I do know, however, is that without him I'd be utterly lost.

James Bowen, London, May 2013

For the latest news, stories and pictures from
James and Bob, follow them on Twitter at
www.twitter.com/streetcatbob,
or visit their Facebook page at
www.facebook.com/streetcatbob.

BOB
No Ordinary Cat

JAMES BOWEN

WITH EXCLUSIVE NEW PHOTOS

A SPECIAL ADAPTATION FROM THE BESTSELLING *A STREET CAT NAMED BOB*

'It is moving and life-affirming. Everyone should read this.'
Daily Telegraph

James Bowen was a homeless musician, busking on the streets of London to survive. But the moment he met an injured stray cat with ginger fur and big green eyes, his life began to change. Together James and Bob the cat faced the world – and won.

A special edition for children aged 11 and above of the number one bestseller A Street Cat Named Bob.

A Street Cat Named Bob

JAMES BOWEN

THE NO.1 BESTSELLER

HOW ONE MAN AND HIS CAT FOUND
HOPE ON THE STREETS

'A heart-warming tale with a message of hope'
Daily Mail

'An instantly bestselling memoir that, beside its
heart-warming tale of their friendship, offers an insight
into the injustice of life on the streets that's by turns
frustrating and life-affirming.'
The Times

The moving, uplifting true story of an unlikely
friendship between a man on the streets and the ginger
cat who adopts him and helps him heal his life.